SPIRITUAL ADOPTION:
THE PATH TO SPIRITUAL MATURITY

BY

R. P. ASCANO, Ph.D., D.P.Min.
AND
S. L. ASCANO, D.B.S.

Intermedia Publishing Group

Spiritual Adoption

Published by:
Intermedia Publishing Group, Inc.
P.O. Box 2825
Peoria, Arizona 85380
www.intermedia pub.com

ISBN 978-1-935906-37-7

THIS BOOK IS DEDICATED TO OUR MOTHERS:

My mother, Herminia Ascano, who taught me the meaning of sacrifice for the sake of the family.

Helen Ramos, my adopted spiritual mother who showed me the importance of intercessory prayer.

Ursula Brady, my adopted spiritual mother who gave biblical meaning to uncritical acceptance.

I am indeed indebted to all of you.

R. P. Ascano, Ph.D., D.P.Min.

And to my mother, Maryan E. Thomas, the mother of merit, for making a career of motherhood her highest calling and inspiring me to do the same.

I love you Mom.

Sharon L. Ascano, D.B.S.

ACKNOWLEDGEMENTS

Our deepest and sincere gratitude goes to our friend and colleague, Rev. James Levitt, for his willingness in sharing his par excellence biblical insight and theological consultation. Thank you so very much for the opportunity of being able to establish a covenant relationship with you as we work together in sharing the love of our Heavenly Father to the world in obedience to His mandate.

Our gratitude goes to Lisa Cook for her willingness to give us her perspective, input, and encouragement.

Most of all, our appreciation to our children, Autumn and Micah, who have given us the greatest joy, the privilege of being parents.

CONTENTS

Chapter 1

Attachment Types
Childhood Bitter Roots Impact Adult Relationships

Hebrews 12:15
See to it that no one misses the grace of God and
that no bitter root grows up to cause trouble
and defile many.

People have a tremendous hunger for intimate, nurturing relationships. This desperate need for love is shared by young and old, and by Christians and non-Christians alike. Early relationships with parents and siblings play a crucial role in how people relate to others throughout their lives.

Persons experiencing emotional deprivation, neglect or abuse—either physical or sexual—tend to develop some type of personality disorder. These people want love, but they are afraid of intimate, nurturing relationships. Adults who have had no single traumatic event in their lives, but were exposed to inconsistent or unresponsive parenting, may also experience a form of attachment disorder. A perfect example would be latchkey children. These are a generation of children who had minimal and/or inconsistent parenting. In order to survive, these children learned that they could only depend on themselves. Consequently, their sense of hyper-independence led to a self-centered "my way" attitude. As these children became adults, they had difficulty submitting to authority figures.

This fear of submission follows them throughout life, in their relationships at home, work, church, and even into their relationship with God. The sense of an ambivalent relationship or "double-mindedness" (James 1:6-7) hinders their spiritual growth and maturity. "Bearing the fruit of the Spirit" (Gal. 5:25-27) becomes an impossible goal, because they lack a spiritual, nurturing relationship with a parental figure. If God truly created humanity due to His desire for fellowship, and man is created in His image, then mankind has a need for fellowship. Maturity may not be able to be achieved without re-parenting.

A child's attachment disorder affects the entire family dynamic. Sibling relationships tend to be conflictual due to this child's need for full attention from the primary parent. Any attention given to other siblings is perceived as a threat to his own emotional need for nurturance. When the primary parent is not providing the requisite attention this child has the tendency to create crisis to acquire the necessary attention. This child is a significant source of emotional exhaustion to the parent. Frequently, the primary parent will feel a sense of profound guilt due to having thoughts of rejection toward this child. When this child perceives any behavioral indication of rejection or distancing by the parent either the child will regress, manifesting immature behavior, clinging to the parent manifesting acute separation anxiety, or will exhibit intense behavioral problems.

The following Scriptures reflect the necessity of being subjected to a higher authority.

Subjection to Higher Authorities

A. God is Over All Authorities Submission is required of everyone.	Romans 13:1-7 Everyone must submit himself to the governing authorities, for there is no authority except that which God has established. The authorities that exist have been established by God. [2]Consequently, he who rebels against the authority is rebelling against what God has instituted, and those who do so will bring judgment on themselves. [3]For rulers hold no terror for those who do right, but for those who do wrong. Do you want to be free from fear of the one in authority? Then do what is right and he will commend you. [4]For he is God's servant to do you good. But if you do wrong, be afraid, for he does not bear the sword for nothing. He is God's servant, an agent of wrath to bring punishment on the wrongdoer. [5]Therefore, it is necessary to submit to the authorities, not only because of possible punishment but also because of conscience. [6]This is also why you pay taxes, for the authorities are God's servants, who give their full time to governing. [7]Give everyone what you owe him: If you owe taxes, pay taxes;

	if revenue, then revenue; if respect, then respect; if honor, then honor.
All authorities are subjected to Christ.	Colossians 2:9-10 For in Christ all the fullness of the Deity lives in bodily form, [10]and you have been given fullness in Christ, who is the head over every power and authority.
B. Disobedience is Linked With Following Our Sinful, Corrupt Nature Corrupt behavior is linked with despising authority.	2 Peter 2:9-11 If this is so, then the Lord knows how to rescue godly men from trials and to hold the unrighteous for the day of judgment, while continuing their punishment. [10]This is especially true of those who follow the corrupt desire of the sinful nature and despise authority. Bold and arrogant, these men are not afraid to slander celestial beings; [11]yet even angels, although they are stronger and more powerful, do not bring slanderous accusations against such beings in the presence of the Lord. Jude 1:7-8 In a similar way, Sodom and Gomorrah and the surrounding towns gave themselves up to sexual immorality and

	perversion. They serve as an example of those who suffer the punishment of eternal fire. [8]In the very same way, these dreamers pollute their own bodies, reject authority and slander celestial beings
Rejecting authority is linked to a sinful life.	1 Timothy 1:18-19 Timothy, my son, I give you this instruction in keeping with the prophecies once made about you, so that by following them you may fight the good fight, [19]holding on to faith and a good conscience. Some have rejected these and so have shipwrecked their faith. Romans 13:2 Consequently, he who rebels against the authority is rebelling against what God has instituted, and those who do so will bring judgment on themselves.
C. Submission is for the Lord's Sake To obey every authority is not to keep a believer in bondage; it is to show respect for the person in authority and to show respect to God.	1 Peter 2:13-17 Submit yourselves for the Lord's sake to every authority instituted among men: whether to the king, as the supreme authority, [14]or to governors, who are sent by him to punish those who do wrong and to commend

those who do right. [15]For it is God's will that by doing good you should silence the ignorant talk of foolish men. [16]Live as free men, but do not use your freedom as a cover-up for evil; live as servants of God. [17]Show proper respect to everyone: Love the brotherhood of believers, fear God, honor the king.

D. Why it's Advantageous to Submit

Authority within the church is not only to keep order, but also to build each other up. This authority may be indicative of the authority to discipline so that maturation can take place.

2 Corinthians 13:10

This is why I write these things when I am absent, that when I come I may not have to be harsh in my use of authority—the authority the Lord gave me for building you up, not for tearing you down.

1 Corinthians 14:33

For God is not a God of disorder but of peace. As in all the congregations of the saints,

The believer's responsibility to those in authority is to pray for them, the advantages are peace, godliness, holiness and a quiet life.

1 Timothy 2:1-2

I urge, then, first of all, that requests, prayers, intercession and thanksgiving be made for everyone — [2]for kings and all those in authority, that we may live peaceful and quiet lives in all godliness and holiness.

It would be disadvantageous for the believer not to obey.	Hebrews 13:17 Obey your leaders and submit to their authority. They keep watch over you as men who must give an account. Obey them so that their work will be a joy, not a burden, for that would be of no advantage to you.
To obey Jesus' commands equals a good reputation.	1 Timothy 6:13-14 In the sight of God, who gives life to everything, and of Christ Jesus, who while testifying before Pontius Pilate made the good confession, I charge you [14]to keep this command without spot or blame until the appearing of our Lord Jesus Christ,

Bonding and attachment are directional. Bonding refers to the relationship as viewed from the parent to the child; attachment refers to the relationship as viewed by the child to the parent. The concept of attachment theory was developed by Mary Salter Ainsworth, John Bowlby, and James Robertson.[1, 2, 3] According to their psychological construct, in order to become healthy adults, children need consistent nurturing, comfort, and support from parents or parental figures.

1   M. Ainsworth and J. Bowlby, "Research strategy in the study of mother-child separation," *Courrier De La Centre International De l'Enfance* 4 (1954).

2   J. Bowlby, "Some pathological processes set in train by early mother-child separation," *Journal of Mental Science* 99 (1953).

3   J. Robertson and J. Bowlby, "Responses of young children to separation from their mothers," *Courrier De La Centre International De l'Enfance* 2 (1952).

Eighty percent of children who are abused or neglected in the first year of life show symptoms of Reactive Attachment Disorder.[4] Reactive Attachment Disorder consists of inappropriate developmental social responses including inhibition, hypervigilance, which is an increase in awareness of one's physical and social environment, resistance to comforting, and indiscriminate attachments. Beverly James proposes that the children who were traumatized physically and sexually are the same children who have attachment disorders.[5] With reports of child abuse in the United States having increased steadily by 4 to 17 percent each year since 1983,[6] this has caused an increase in the number of people who have attachment disorders.

Developing trust is based on consistently meeting an infant's physical and emotional needs. Meeting these needs enables spiritual development. This concept can be seen in Scripture.

James 2:15-16

Suppose a brother or sister is without clothes and daily food. [16]If one of you says to him, "Go, I wish you well; keep warm and well fed," but does nothing about his physical needs, what good is it?

---

4 D. Cicchetti and D. Barnett, "Attachment organization in maltreated preschoolers," *Development and Psychopathology* 3 (1991).

5 B. James, *Handbook for treatment of attachment-trauma problems in children* (New York: Free Press, 1994).

6 P. Pecora, J. Whittaker and A. Maluccio, *The child welfare challenge: Policy, practice, and research* (New York: Walter de Gruyter, Inc., 1992).

Developing Trust

A. Having Basic Needs Met Leads to Trust Development of trust occurs when infants' basic needs are met. David's basic need for food and touch were being met and this translated into trusting God.	Psalm 22:9-10 Yet you brought me out of the womb you made me trust in you even at my mother's breast. [10]From birth I was cast upon you; from my mother's womb you have been my God. Psalm 71:6 From birth I have relied on you; you brought me forth from my mother's womb. I will ever praise you.
God took care of the Israelites' physical needs first so they would understand that He was their God. Then they were ready to have their spiritual needs met when God poured out His spirit.	Joel 2:25-29 "I will repay you for the years the locusts have eaten—the great locust and the young locust, the other locusts and the locust swarm—my great army that I sent among you. [26]You will have plenty to eat, until you are full, and you will praise the name of the Lord your God, who has worked wonders for you; never again will my people be shamed. [27]Then you will know that I am in Israel, that I am the Lord your God, and that there is no other; never again will my people be shamed. [28] "And afterward, I will pour out my Spirit on all people.

Your sons and daughters will prophesy, your old men will dream dreams, your young men will see visions. [29]Even on my servants, both men and women, I will pour out my Spirit in those days.

God first took care of Elijah's physical needs. Then Elijah was able to have a conversation with God.

1 Kings 19:3-13

Elijah was afraid and ran for his life. When he came to Beersheba in Judah, he left his servant there, [4]while he himself went a day's journey into the desert. He came to a broom tree, sat down under it and prayed that he might die. "I have had enough, Lord," he said. "Take my life; I am no better than my ancestors." [5]Then he lay down under the tree and fell asleep. All at once an angel touched him and said, "Get up and eat." [6]He looked around, and there by his head was a cake of bread baked over hot coals, and a jar of water. He ate and drank and then lay down again. [7]The angel of the Lord came back a second time and touched him and said, "Get up and eat, for the journey is too much for you." [8]So he got up and ate and drank. Strengthened by that food, he traveled forty days and forty nights until he reached Horeb, the mountain of God. [9]There he went into a cave and spent the night. And the word of the Lord came to him: "What are you doing here, Elijah?" [10]He replied, "I have been very zealous for the Lord God Almighty. The Israelites have rejected your covenant, broken down your altars, and put your prophets to death with the sword. I am the only one left, and now they are trying to kill me too." [11]The Lord said, "Go out and stand on the mountain in the presence of the Lord, for the Lord is about to pass by." Then a great and powerful wind tore the mountains apart and shattered the rocks before the Lord, but the Lord was not in the wind. After the wind there was an earthquake, but the Lord was not in the earthquake. [12]After the earthquake came a fire, but the Lord was not in the fire. And after the fire came a gentle whisper. [13]When Elijah heard it, he pulled his cloak over his face and went out and stood at the mouth of the cave. Then a voice said to him, "What are you doing here, Elijah?"

B. Trust Comes From Consistent Daily Care and Involvement

2 Timothy 3:14-15

But as for you, continue in what you have learned and

Timothy's mother and grandmother enabled him to know the Scriptures from infancy by the way they met his needs and lived out Scripture.

have become convinced of, because you know those from whom you learned it, [15]and how from infancy you have known the holy Scriptures, which are able to make you wise for salvation through faith in Christ Jesus.

Jesus was not in a back room but surrounded by life and activity, visited by shepherds and kings.

Luke 2:15-18

When the angels had left them and gone into heaven, the shepherds said to one another, "Let's go to Bethlehem and see this thing that has happened, which the Lord has told us about." [16]So they hurried off and found Mary and Joseph, and the baby, who was lying in the manger. [17]When they had seen him, they spread the word concerning what had been told them about this child, [18]and all who heard it were amazed at what the shepherds said to them.

Matthew 2:11

On coming to the house, they saw the child with his mother Mary, and they bowed down and worshiped him. Then they opened their treasures and presented him with gifts of gold and of incense and of myrrh.

The children were included in important times of prayer, this was a family event. This does not mean that the small children were expected to kneel quietly. The mothers most likely prayed with their eyes open in order to keep their little ones from eating sand or heading for the water!

When the law was read all who were old enough to understand were there. This would have included at least school age children. The children were not just present physically; they participated by listening attentively, standing, bowing, and worshipping.

Acts 21:5-6

But when our time was up, we left and continued on our way. All the disciples and their wives and children accompanied us out of the city, and there on the beach we knelt to pray. ⁶After saying goodbye to each other, we went aboard the ship, and they returned home.

Nehemiah 8:1-6

all the people assembled as one man in the square before the Water Gate. They told Ezra the scribe to bring out the Book of the Law of Moses, which the Lord had commanded for Israel. ²So on the first day of the seventh month Ezra the priest brought the Law before the assembly, which was made up of men and women and all who were able to understand. ³He read it aloud from daybreak till noon as he faced the square before the Water Gate in the presence of the men, women and others who could understand. And all the people listened attentively to the Book of the Law. ⁴Ezra the scribe stood on a high wooden platform built for the occasion. Beside him on his right stood Mattithiah, Shema, Anaiah,

	Uriah, Hilkiah and Maaseiah; and on his left were Pedaiah, Mishael, Malkijah, Hashum, Hashbaddanah, Zechariah and Meshullam. [5]Ezra opened the book. All the people could see him because he was standing above them; and as he opened it, the people all stood up. [6]Ezra praised the Lord, the great God; and all the people lifted their hands and responded, "Amen! Amen!" Then they bowed down and worshiped the Lord with their faces to the ground.
Even at a solemn fast infants and children were included.	Joel 2:15-16 Blow the trumpet in Zion, declare a holy fast, call a sacred assembly. [16]Gather the people, consecrate the assembly; bring together the elders, gather the children, those nursing at the breast. Let the bridegroom leave his room and the bride her chamber.
C. Comfort is a Basic Need God sees comfort as a basic parenting skill. Being comforted is as important as food.	Isaiah 66:13 As a mother comforts her child, so will I comfort you; and you will be comforted over Jerusalem." 1 Thessalonians 2:6-9 We were not looking for praise from men, not from you or

	anyone else. As apostles of Christ we could have been a burden to you, [7]but we were gentle among you, like a mother caring for her little children. [8]We loved you so much that we were delighted to share with you not only the gospel of God but our lives as well, because you had become so dear to us. [9]Surely you remember, brothers, our toil and hardship; we worked night and day in order not to be a burden to anyone while we preached the gospel of God to you. 1 Thessalonians 2:11-12 For you know that we dealt with each of you as a father deals with his own children, [12]encouraging, comforting and urging you to live lives worthy of God, who calls you into his kingdom and glory.

Lack of consistent care giving from parents may result in different levels of relationship attachment styles as the child becomes an adult. Research data indicates different levels of attachment, such as secure base, anxious ambivalent, avoidant, and disorganized.

Attachment

SECURE BASE ATTACHMENT Secure base attachment is typically associated with consistent and responsive nurturing from parents. As an adult, someone who received this type of care relates well to others and has the capacity for warm, nurturing, and caring interactions. People with a secure base attachment have positive self-worth, self-esteem, and self-confidence. They are able to be open and engage in meaningful interaction. More importantly, these individuals can receive feedback without feeling profoundly threatened. They are teachable.	Proverbs 1:2-6 for attaining wisdom and discipline; for understanding words of insight; ³for acquiring a disciplined and prudent life, doing what is right and just and fair; ⁴for giving prudence to the simple, knowledge and discretion to the young— ⁵let the wise listen and add to their learning, and let the discerning get guidance— ⁶for understanding proverbs and parables, the sayings and riddles of the wise.
Timothy is a good example of secure base attachment. Even though Timothy had a secure base attachment to his mother and grandmother, his father was not a believer. Timothy needed Paul as a spiritual father. Children need attachment to both parents. With attachment to only one parent, spiritual parenting from a spiritual adoptive parent is warranted.	Acts 16:1 He came to Derbe and then to Lystra, where a disciple named Timothy lived, whose mother was a Jewess and a believer, but whose father was a Greek. 1 Timothy 1:2 To Timothy my true son in the faith: Grace, mercy and peace from God the Father and Christ Jesus our Lord.

| Naomi adopted Ruth as an adult. | Ruth 1:18
When Naomi realized that Ruth was determined to go with her, she stopped urging her. |
| **ANXIOUS AMBIVALENT**
A person with an anxious ambivalent style of attachment received inconsistent and intermittent parenting. Individuals in this category tend to be insecure, prone to co-dependent relationships, have low frustration tolerance, and are morbidly preoccupied with their needs. Because of their insecurity, they tend to demand fairness in all aspects of life. Fairness is a perception. A child's perspective on fairness will color his perception on his parents' love. This will affect his perception of siblings as well. As adults, when such people are involved in a ministry, they may complain to God about their predicaments. Jonah's response to God is an example of demanding fairness. | Jonah 4:1-11
But Jonah was greatly displeased and became angry. [2]He prayed to the Lord, "O Lord, is this not what I said when I was still at home? That is why I was so quick to flee to Tarshish. I knew that you are a gracious and compassionate God, slow to anger and abounding in love, a God who relents from sending calamity. [3]Now, O Lord, take away my life, for it is better for me to die than to live." [4]But the Lord replied, "Have you any right to be angry?" [5]Jonah went out and sat down at a place east of the city. There he made himself a shelter, sat in its shade and waited to see what would happen to the city. [6]Then the Lord God provided a vine and made it grow up over Jonah to give shade for his head to ease his discomfort, and Jonah was very happy about the vine. [7]But at dawn the next day God provided a worm, which chewed the vine so that it withered. [8]When the sun rose, God provided a scorching east wind, and the sun blazed on Jonah's head so |

that he grew faint. He wanted to die, and said, "It would be better for me to die than to live." ⁹But God said to Jonah, "Do you have a right to be angry about the vine?" "I do," he said. "I am angry enough to die." ¹⁰But the Lord said, "You have been concerned about this vine, though you did not tend it or make it grow. It sprang up overnight and died overnight. ¹¹But Nineveh has more than a hundred and twenty thousand people who cannot tell their right hand from their left, and many cattle as well. Should I not be concerned about that great city?"

AVOIDANT

The next type of attachment style is avoidant. As infants, and most likely throughout their developmental and formative years, these people received unresponsive and/or neglectful parenting. As adults, they are hypersensitive, inhibited, feel inadequate, and seek to protect themselves through privacy. They may become hermits. As a response to painful isolation and loneliness in childhood, they worry over their sense of emptiness. They vacillate between the desire

2 Kings 11:1-5

When Athaliah the mother of Ahaziah saw that her son was dead, she proceeded to destroy the whole royal family. ²But Jehosheba, the daughter of King Jehoram and sister of Ahaziah, took Joash son of Ahaziah and stole him away from among the royal princes, who were about to be murdered. She put him and his nurse in a bedroom to hide him from Athaliah; so he was not killed. ³He remained hidden with his nurse at the temple of the Lord for six years while Athaliah ruled the land. ⁴In the seventh year Jehoiada

for affection and the fear of showing emotion. Joash experienced the death of his father when he was an infant and experienced the trauma of his mother attempting to kill him. He was kept hidden for six years by his aunt. His mother was executed and Joash became king at the age of seven. Jehoiada, the high priest, gave him council and Joash followed it and did right. However, when Jehoiada died at the age of 130 years Joash followed the officials of Judah and abandoned the temple of the Lord. Joash was eventually assassinated. Avoidant types tend to be insecure; they lack self-worth and social skills. Their fear of rejection makes decision making difficult so they tend to acquiesce to the influence of others.

sent for the commanders of units of a hundred, the Carites and the guards and had them brought to him at the temple of the Lord. He made a covenant with them and put them under oath at the temple of the Lord. Then he showed them the king's son. ⁵He commanded them, saying, "This is what you are to do: You who are in the three companies that are going on duty on the Sabbath—a third of you guarding the royal palace,

2 Kings 12:2

Joash did what was right in the eyes of the Lord all the years Jehoiada the priest instructed him.

2 Chronicles 24:15-25

Now Jehoiada was old and full of years, and he died at the age of a hundred and thirty. ¹⁶He was buried with the kings in the City of David, because of the good he had done in Israel for God and his temple. ¹⁷After the death of Jehoiada, the officials of Judah came and paid homage to the king, and he listened to them. ¹⁸They abandoned the temple of the Lord, the God of their fathers, and worshiped Asherah poles and idols. Because of their guilt, God's anger came upon Judah and

Jerusalem. [19]Although the Lord sent prophets to the people to bring them back to him, and though they testified against them, they would not listen. [20]Then the Spirit of God came upon Zechariah son of Jehoiada the priest. He stood before the people and said, "This is what God says: 'Why do you disobey the Lord's commands? You will not prosper. Because you have forsaken the Lord, he has forsaken you.'" [21]But they plotted against him, and by order of the king they stoned him to death in the courtyard of the Lord's temple. [22]King Joash did not remember the kindness Zechariah's father Jehoiada had shown him but killed his son, who said as he lay dying, "May the Lord see this and call you to account." [23]At the turn of the year, the army of Aram marched against Joash; it invaded Judah and Jerusalem and killed all the leaders of the people. They sent all the plunder to their king in Damascus. [24]Although the Aramean army had come with only a few men, the Lord delivered into their hands a much larger army. Because Judah had forsaken the Lord, the God of their fathers, judgment was executed on Joash. [25]When the Arameans withdrew, they left Joash severely wounded.

	His officials conspired against him for murdering the son of Jehoiada the priest, and they killed him in his bed. So he died and was buried in the City of David, but not in the tombs of the kings.
God does not want people to be isolated.	**Acts 2:42** They devoted themselves to the apostles' teaching and to the fellowship, to the breaking of bread and to prayer. **Acts 2:46** Every day they continued to meet together in the temple courts. They broke bread in their homes and ate together with glad and sincere hearts, **Hebrews 10:24-25** And let us consider how we may spur one another on toward love and good deeds. 25Let us not give up meeting together, as some are in the habit of doing, but let us encourage one another—and all the more as you see the Day approaching.
God did not want Elijah to think he was alone.	**1 Kings 19:14-18** He replied, "I have been very zealous for the Lord God Almighty. The Israelites have rejected your covenant, broken down your altars, and put your

prophets to death with the sword. I am the only one left, and now they are trying to kill me too." ¹⁵The Lord said to him, "Go back the way you came, and go to the Desert of Damascus. When you get there, anoint Hazael king over Aram. ¹⁶Also, anoint Jehu son of Nimshi king over Israel, and anoint Elisha son of Shaphat from Abel Meholah to succeed you as prophet. ¹⁷Jehu will put to death any who escape the sword of Hazael, and Elisha will put to death any who escape the sword of Jehu. ¹⁸Yet I reserve seven thousand in Israel—all whose knees have not bowed down to Baal and all whose mouths have not kissed him."

DISORGANIZED ATTACHMENT

The last category is the disorganized attachment style. These people were criticized and rejected as children, and possibly experienced a traumatic event. As adults, they may be violent, aggressive, impulsive, egocentric, lack empathy for others, and display a grandiose sense of self worth. Saul exemplifies this when he rationalized his behavior even

1 Samuel 15:10-21

Then the word of the Lord came to Samuel: ¹¹"I am grieved that I have made Saul king, because he has turned away from me and has not carried out my instructions." Samuel was troubled, and he cried out to the Lord all that night.

¹²Early in the morning Samuel got up and went to meet Saul, but he was told, "Saul has gone to Carmel. There he has set up a monument in his own honor and has turned and gone

when Samuel confronted him directly with his disobedience.	on down to Gilgal." [13]When Samuel reached him, Saul said, "The Lord bless you! I have carried out the Lord's instructions." [14]But Samuel said, "What then is this bleating of sheep in my ears? What is this lowing of cattle that I hear?" [15]Saul answered, "The soldiers brought them from the Amalekites; they spared the best of the sheep and cattle to sacrifice to the Lord your God, but we totally destroyed the rest." [16]"Stop!" Samuel said to Saul. "Let me tell you what the Lord said to me last night." "Tell me," Saul replied. [17]Samuel said, "Although you were once small in your own eyes, did you not become the head of the tribes of Israel? The Lord anointed you king over Israel. [18]And he sent you on a mission, saying, 'Go and completely destroy those wicked people, the Amalekites; make war on them until you have wiped them out.' [19]Why did you not obey the Lord? Why did you pounce on the plunder and do evil in the eyes of the Lord?" [20]"But I did obey the Lord," Saul said. "I went on the mission the Lord assigned me. I completely destroyed the Amalekites and brought back Agag their king. [21]The soldiers took sheep and cattle from the

plunder, the best of what was devoted to God, in order to sacrifice them to the Lord your God at Gilgal."

Self-worth does not come from who our parents are, but from who created us.

Job 31:13-15

"If I have denied justice to my menservants and maidservants when they had a grievance against me, ¹⁴what will I do when God confronts me? What will I answer when called to account? ¹⁵Did not he who made me in the womb make them? Did not the same one form us both within our mothers?

God knows how important it is to provide a secure relationship with His people. He promises not to abandon His children, either physically or psychologically.

Deuteronomy 4:31

For the Lord your God is a merciful God; he will not abandon or destroy you or forget the covenant with your forefathers, which he confirmed to them by oath.

1 Kings 6:13

And I will live among the Israelites and will not abandon my people Israel."

Nehemiah 9:19

"Because of your great compassion you did not abandon them in the desert. By day the pillar of cloud did not cease to guide them on their path, nor the pillar of fire by

	night to shine on the way they were to take."
	Nehemiah 9:31 But in your great mercy you did not put an end to them or abandon them, for you are a gracious and merciful God.
	Hebrews 13:5 Keep your lives free from the love of money and be content with what you have, because God has said, "Never will I leave you; never will I forsake you."
	John 14:18 I will not leave you as orphans; I will come to you.

Children who develop symptoms of attachment disorder are unable to respond appropriately to most social situations. They find it difficult to form close friendships and submit to authority, both in school and in their social lives. In the same way these children will have difficulty relating to God unless they are re-parented. Those with avoidant attachment pray less than those who are nonavoidant, even in times of stress, whereas, anxious attachment individuals prayed more petitionary prayers.[7] Mentoring is not enough. Because they are accustomed to unstable parenting, these children fear and resist being comforted. They may react in a passive aggressive manner to nurturing. The implications to the ministry cannot be ignored:

---

7   K. R. Byrd, and A. Boe, "The correspondence between attachment dimensions and prayer in
    college students," *International Journal for the Psychology of Religion* 11 (2001).

- Attachment disorders in childhood affects adult adjustment
- Maladjusted adults become dysfunctional parents
- People with psychological disorders impact the spiritual health of an entire congregation, as well as the community

People with attachment disorders not only suffer psychological problems, but may have physical symptoms as well. In 1985, van der Kolk, Greenberg, Boyd, and Krystal proposed that trauma produced changes in the central nervous system.[8] Changing norepinephrine levels in the brain led to diminished motivation, hyperactive behavior, and unstable emotions.[9] Growing evidence shows that severe, chronic stress early in life leads to long-term effects on the body—specifically with the glands that govern the response to stress. Three glands control the release of stress hormones in response to physical and psychological emergencies: the hypothalamus, the pituitary, and the adrenal glands. People with major depression usually have changes in these glands. The work of Paul McLean suggests that traumatic events are encoded directly to the limbic system which is the brain's emotional center.[10]

The fact that both physical and emotional changes occur after traumatic events, such as in Posttraumatic Stress Disorder patients, reinforces the premise that Christians need to focus on re-parenting as well as interceding for emotional *and* physical healing. One of the primary consequences of experiencing a traumatic event is living in an acute state of alertness and anticipatory fear that produces stress hormones, facilitating neurodeterioration and weakening the immune system, thus increasing the victims' susceptibility to psychogenic illness. Fear evokes pessimism, which in turn negatively impacts trust relationships. Reestablishment of a trusting and reciprocal nurturing relationship is essential in restoring an individual to psychophysiological and spiritual health. Understanding the problems that underlie attachment disorders will help Christians do more than address the symptoms. Instead of reacting to surface behavior, they can be proactive in providing love and care for hurting children.

---

8 B. van der Kolk, M. Greenberg, H. Boyd, and J. Krystal, "Inescapable shock, neurotransmitters, and addictions to trauma: Toward a psychology of posttraumatic stress," *Biological Psychiatry* 20 (1985).

9 B. van der Kolk, M. Greenberg, H. Boyd, and J. Krystal, "Inescapable shock, neurotransmitters, and addictions to trauma: Toward a psychology of posttraumatic stress," *Biological Psychiatry* 20 (1985).

10 P. McLean, *The Triune Brain in Evolution,* (New York: Plenum Press, 1990).

Chapter 2

Spiritual Consequences:
Secure Base Attachment

Our ability to form a covenant relationship with God is based on our capacity to enter into secure base attachments. Such relationships are the opposite of attachment disorder.

Secure Base Attachment

God is relational; He chooses His children and that brings Him pleasure. Adopted children need to know that they were chosen. The only way to become a part of God's family is to be adopted.	**Ephesians 1:4-5** For he chose us in him before the creation of the world to be holy and blameless in his sight. In love ⁵he predestined us to be adopted as his sons through Jesus Christ, in accordance with his pleasure and will— **1 Corinthians 1:9** God, who has called you into fellowship with his Son Jesus Christ our Lord, is faithful.
Believers cannot have true fellowship with one another unless they first have fellowship with God. If attachment to Him is not secure, then relationships	**1 John 1:3-7** We proclaim to you what we have seen and heard, so that you also may have fellowship with us. And our fellowship is with the Father and with his Son,

with others will not be secure. Without re-parenting, people with attachment disorders will not be able to maximize their fellowship with God or others. Fellowship with God is evident in the way believers live.

Just as becoming devoted to teaching and prayer takes effort, so does devotion to fellowship. It is much easier for the person with an attachment disorder to remain isolated.

Jesus Christ. [4]We write this to make our joy complete. [5]This is the message we have heard from him and declare to you: God is light; in him there is no darkness at all. [6]If we claim to have fellowship with him yet walk in the darkness, we lie and do not live by the truth. [7]But if we walk in the light, as he is in the light, we have fellowship with one another, and the blood of Jesus, his Son, purifies us from all sin.

Acts 2:42
They devoted themselves to the apostles' teaching and to the fellowship, to the breaking of bread and to prayer.

Hebrews 10:24-25
And let us consider how we may spur one another on toward love and good deeds. [25]Let us not give up meeting together, as some are in the habit of doing, but let us encourage one another—and all the more as you see the Day approaching.

General literature on attachment indicates that the nature of the parent/child relationship is critical in developing an adult capacity for empathy that will eventually lead to intimacy.

Attachment theory provides insight into how interpersonal relationships work—or don't work. People who have established a secure base attachment are basically stable and have the innate capacity to form reciprocal relationships without difficulty. They are also able to have an intimate relationship with God. These people are able to share the blessings they receive from God and are sensitive to the needs of others. They are able to form close friendships, (both platonic and loving), and sustain these friendships. These people can access childhood memories—both positive and negative—without fixating on their experiences. Unpleasant events in their lives have been psychospiritually processed and do not hinder their ability to build strong relationships with God and their fellow man. They seek appropriate support systems (horizontal relationships). They are flexible, resilient under psychological duress, and able to establish their identity with Christ Jesus.

An example of secure base attachment can be seen with the young daughter of a missionary couple. In 2003 an urgent call came from a psychologist for a crisis management consultation. This psychologist was the primary clinical consultant for a large denomination and was counseling a ten-year-old child after the death of her missionary family. The father, mother, and her brother were killed; she was the only survivor of this tragedy. She had been brutally choked into unconsciousness and raped. Her story reflects a secure base attachment legacy from her parents, who themselves had secure base attachment from their parents.

The girl's grandmother went to the jail and told the man who murdered her son, daughter-in-law, and grandson that she forgave him. At the funeral, she called the mother of the murderer up to the front and said they were both mothers grieving for lost sons. She implored the community to remove any shroud of blame from the family, specifically the mother. When the surviving child was asked where she wanted to live, she indicated she wanted to stay in the community where her family was killed. Because that was not a viable option, she promised to come back someday as a missionary.

Our Identity in Christ

If this intimacy is not attained with other people, it will be difficult to obtain with God.	1 John 4:20 If anyone says, "I love God," yet hates his brother, he is a liar. For anyone who does not love his brother, whom he has seen, cannot love God, whom he has not seen.
Affirm an identity with Christ by acknowledging the following:	
I am God's child.	John 1:12 Yet to all who received him, to those who believed in his name, he gave the right to become children of God—
I am Christ's friend.	John 15:15 I no longer call you servants, because a servant does not know his master's business. Instead, I have called you friends, for everything that I learned from my Father I have made known to you.
I have been justified.	Romans 5:1 Therefore, since we have been justified through faith, we have peace with God through our Lord Jesus Christ,
I am united with the Lord.	1 Corinthians 6:17 But he who unites himself with the Lord is one with him in spirit.

I am a member of Christ's body.	1 Corinthians 12:27 Now you are the body of Christ, and each one of you is a part of it.
I am a saint.	Ephesians 1:1 Paul, an apostle of Christ Jesus by the will of God, to the saints in Ephesus, the faithful in Christ Jesus:
I am complete in Christ.	Colossians 2:10 and you have been given fullness in Christ, who is the head over every power and authority.

Biblical characters provide fascinating examples of different types of relationships and attachments. The type of parenting or upbringing these men and women received is not always known, but their personality traits and behavior provide clues to various types of attachment.

Biblical Examples of Secure Base Attachment

| Daniel was a problem solver. People with a secure base attachment are more capable of problem solving than those without a secure base attachment. | Daniel 1:8
But Daniel resolved not to defile himself with the royal food and wine, and he asked the chief official for permission not to defile himself this way.

Daniel 1:11-14
Daniel then said to the guard whom the chief official had appointed over Daniel, |

Hananiah, Mishael and Azariah, [12]"Please test your servants for ten days: Give us nothing but vegetables to eat and water to drink. [13]Then compare our appearance with that of the young men who eat the royal food, and treat your servants in accordance with what you see." [14]So he agreed to this and tested them for ten days.

Daniel was faithful, honest, and always responsible. Though kidnapped as a teen, he showed traits of secure base attachment and resiliency.

Daniel 6:4

At this, the administrators and the satraps tried to find grounds for charges against Daniel in his conduct of government affairs, but they were unable to do so. They could find no corruption in him, because he was trustworthy and neither corrupt nor negligent.

Daniel sought others to pray with him. Individuals with a secure base attachment are willing and able to recruit a support system.

Daniel 2:13-19

So the decree was issued to put the wise men to death, and men were sent to look for Daniel and his friends to put them to death. [14]When Arioch, the commander of the king's guard, had gone out to put to death the wise men of Babylon, Daniel spoke to him with wisdom and tact. [15]He asked the king's officer, "Why did the king issue such a harsh decree?" Arioch then explained the matter to Daniel.

¹⁶At this, Daniel went in to the king and asked for time, so that he might interpret the dream for him. ¹⁷Then Daniel returned to his house and explained the matter to his friends Hananiah, Mishael and Azariah. ¹⁸He urged them to plead for mercy from the God of heaven concerning this mystery, so that he and his friends might not be executed with the rest of the wise men of Babylon. ¹⁹During the night the mystery was revealed to Daniel in a vision. Then Daniel praised the God of heaven

Daniel did what was right in spite of the consequences. A secure base attached individual has a greater capacity for moral integrity.

Daniel 6:7-10

The royal administrators, prefects, satraps, advisers and governors have all agreed that the king should issue an edict and enforce the decree that anyone who prays to any god or man during the next thirty day, except to you, O king, shall be thrown into the lions' den. ⁸Now, O king, issue the decree and put it in writing so that it cannot be altered—in accordance with the laws of the Medes and Persians, which cannot be repealed." ⁹So King Darius put the decree in writing. ¹⁰Now when Daniel learned that the decree had been published, he went home to his upstairs room where

A parent can establish a secure base attachment with one child and not others. This explains how one child from the same family can depart from the family's teaching and spiritual heritage. David's son, Solomon, exhibited characteristics of secure base attachment. In spite of the fact that Solomon's parents' relationship started with lust and the murder of Uriah, his father David repented. In doing so, he broke what might have become a generational sin. However, because of the behavior of two of David's other sons it does not appear that David broke the generational curses that affected his sons Amnon, whose mother was Ahinoam, and Absalom, whose mother was Maacah.

the windows opened toward Jerusalem. Three times a day he got down on his knees and prayed, giving thanks to his God, just as he had done before.

2 Samuel 12:16-25
David pleaded with God for the child. He fasted and went into his house and spent the nights lying on the ground. [17]The elders of his household stood beside him to get him up from the ground, but he refused, and he would not eat any food with them. [18]On the seventh day the child died. David's servants were afraid to tell him that the child was dead, for they thought, "While the child was still living, we spoke to David but he would not listen to us. How can we tell him the child is dead? He may do something desperate." [19]David noticed that his servants were whispering among themselves and he realized the child was dead. "Is the child dead?" he asked. "Yes," they replied, "he is dead." [20]Then David got up from the ground. After he had washed, put on lotions and changed his clothes, he went into the house of the Lord and worshiped. Then he went to his own house, and at his request

they served him food, and he ate. [21]His servants asked him, "Why are you acting this way? While the child was alive, you fasted and wept, but now that the child is dead, you get up and eat!" [22]He answered, "While the child was still alive, I fasted and wept. I thought, 'Who knows? The Lord may be gracious to me and let the child live.' [23]But now that he is dead, why should I fast? Can I bring him back again? I will go to him, but he will not return to me." [24]Then David comforted his wife Bathsheba, and he went to her and lay with her. She gave birth to a son, and they named him Solomon. The Lord loved him; [25]and because the Lord loved him, he sent word through Nathan the prophet to name him Jedidiah.

Solomon's brother, Adonijah, caused problems by setting himself up as king. A man like Solomon who exhibited secure base attachment could still act in a dysfunctional way; the product of original sin manifesting itself through his multiple wives and worship of other gods.

1 Kings 1:50-53
But Adonijah, in fear of Solomon, went and took hold of the horns of the altar. [51]Then Solomon was told, "Adonijah is afraid of King Solomon and is clinging to the horns of the altar. He says, 'Let King Solomon swear to me today that he will not put his servant to death with the sword.'" [52]Solomon replied, "If he shows himself to be a worthy man, not

a hair of his head will fall to the ground; but if evil is found in him, he will die." [53]Then King Solomon sent men, and they brought him down from the altar. And Adonijah came and bowed down to King Solomon, and Solomon said, "Go to your home."

1 Kings 11:1
King Solomon, however, loved many foreign women besides Pharaoh's daughter—
Moabites, Ammonites, Edomites, Sidonians and Hittites.

1 Kings 11:4-5
As Solomon grew old, his wives turned his heart after other gods, and his heart was not fully devoted to the Lord his God, as the heart of David his father had been. [5]He followed Ashtoreth the goddess of the Sidonians, and Molech the detestable god of the Ammonites.

David continued to instruct Solomon even up to the time of David's death. Establishing a secure base in re-parenting is a life-long covenant.

1 Kings 2:1-9
When the time drew near for David to die, he gave a charge to Solomon his son.
[2]"I am about to go the way of all the earth," he said. "So be strong, show yourself a man,

³and observe what the Lord your God requires: Walk in his ways, and keep his decrees and commands, his laws and requirements, as written in the Law of Moses, so that you may prosper in all you do and wherever you go, ⁴and that the Lord may keep his promise to me: 'If your descendants watch how they live, and if they walk faithfully before me with all their heart and soul, you will never fail to have a man on the throne of Israel.' ⁵"Now you yourself know what Joab son of Zeruiah did to me—what he did to the two commanders of Israel's armies, Abner son of Ner and Amasa son of Jether. He killed them, shedding their blood in peacetime as if in battle, and with that blood stained the belt around his waist and the sandals on his feet. ⁶Deal with him according to your wisdom, but do not let his gray head go down to the grave in peace. ⁷"But show kindness to the sons of Barzillai of Gilead and let them be among those who eat at your table. They stood by me when I fled from your brother Absalom. ⁸"And remember, you have with you Shimei son of Gera, the Benjamite from Bahurim, who called down bitter curses on me the day I went to Mahanaim. When he

came down to meet me at the Jordan, I swore to him by the Lord: 'I will not put you to death by the sword.' 9But now, do not consider him innocent. You are a man of wisdom; you will know what to do to him. Bring his gray head down to the grave in blood."

Shadrach, Meshach, and Abednego exhibited traits of secure base attachment. They were willing to learn, and what they learned was filtered through the belief system they acquired during their developmental and formative years. Proverbs 22:6, "Train a child in the way he should go, and when he is old he will not turn from it."

Daniel 1:3-4

Then the king ordered Ashpenaz, chief of his court officials, to bring in some of the Israelites from the royal family and the nobility— 4young men without any physical defect, handsome, showing aptitude for every kind of learning, well informed, quick to understand, and qualified to serve in the king's palace. He was to teach them the language and literature of the Babylonians.

Daniel, Shadrach, Meshach, and Abednego did not lose their identities even though they lost their names. This is a true indication of an established secure base attachment.

Daniel 1:7

The chief official gave them new names: to Daniel, the name Belteshazzar; to Hananiah, Shadrach; to Mishael, Meshach; and to Azariah, Abednego.

They were able to hold leadership positions. Secure base attached individuals are able to maintain their sense of spiritual and emotional commitment to one another.

Daniel 2:49

Moreover, at Daniel's request the king appointed Shadrach, Meshach and Abednego administrators over the province of Babylon, while

They were willing to keep God's commandments in spite of the threat of death. They knew right from wrong and had the ability to stand behind their convictions.

Daniel himself remained at the royal court.

Daniel 3:13-18

Furious with rage, Nebuchadnezzar summoned Shadrach, Meshach and Abednego. So these men were brought before the king, [14]and Nebuchadnezzar said to them, "Is it true, Shadrach, Meshach and Abednego, that you do not serve my gods or worship the image of gold I have set up? [15]Now when you hear the sound of the horn, flute, zither, lyre, harp, pipes and all kinds of music, if you are ready to fall down and worship the image I made, very good. But if you do not worship it, you will be thrown immediately into a blazing furnace. Then what god will be able to rescue you from my hand?" [16]Shadrach, Meshach and Abednego replied to the king, "O Nebuchadnezzar, we do not need to defend ourselves before you in this matter. [17]If we are thrown into the blazing furnace, the God we serve is able to save us from it, and he will rescue us from your hand, O king. [18]But even if he does not, we want you to know, O king, that we will not serve your gods or worship the image of gold you have set up."

The person with a secure base attachment maintains a balanced view of his parents and God. During trials and tribulations, he does not believe God is abandoning, rejecting, or punishing him for misdeeds or unworthiness. When secure base attached people experience psychospiritual duress, they maintain their identities. This is exemplified by the lives of Job and Joseph. Although such people have moments of doubt, in the end the relationship with God remains intact—evidence of psychospiritual resiliency.

Resiliency

Resiliency refers to a constructive rather than destructive reaction to trials and tribulations. With secure base attachment, psychospiritual resiliency becomes evident during times of trials and tribulations.[11] As seen earlier, this was shown by Solomon, Daniel, Shadrach, Meshach, and Abednego. Spiritual resiliency is the natural, self-correcting state of each born again person who receives support (intercessory prayer), nurturing (fellowship), and the opportunity to overcome trials and tribulation. Daniel and Joseph are also examples of reacting to trials constructively as is evidenced by their promotions.

Daniel 2:17-18

Then Daniel returned to his house and explained the matter to his friends Hananiah, Mishael and Azariah. [18]He urged them to plead for mercy from the God of heaven concerning this mystery, so that he and his friends might not be executed with the rest of the wise men of Babylon.

Daniel 1:3-5

Then the king ordered Ashpenaz, chief of his court officials, to bring in some of the Israelites from the royal family and the nobility— [4]young men without any physical defect, handsome, showing aptitude for every kind of learning, well informed, quick to understand, and qualified to serve in the king's palace. He was to teach them the language and

11 S. Luther and G. Cushing, "Measurement issues in the empirical study of resilience: An overview," in *Resilience and development: Positive life adaptations*, ed. M. Glantz and J. Johnson (New York: Plenum Press, 1999).

literature of the Babylonians. [5]The king assigned them a daily amount of food and wine from the king's table. They were to be trained for three years, and after that they were to enter the king's service.

Genesis 37:3

Now Israel loved Joseph more than any of his other sons, because he had been born to him in his old age; and he made a richly ornamented robe for him.

Genesis 39:3-6

When his master saw that the Lord was with him and that the Lord gave him success in everything he did, [4]Joseph found favor in his eyes and became his attendant. Potiphar put him in charge of his household, and he entrusted to his care everything he owned. [5]From the time he put him in charge of his household and of all that he owned, the Lord blessed the household of the Egyptian because of Joseph. The blessing of the Lord was on everything Potiphar had, both in the house and in the field. [6]So he left in Joseph's care everything he had; with Joseph in charge, he did not concern himself with anything except the food he ate. Now Joseph was well-built and handsome,

Genesis 39:20-23

Joseph's master took him and put him in prison, the place where the king's prisoners were confined. But while Joseph was there in the prison, [21]the Lord was with him; he showed him kindness and granted him favor in the eyes of the prison warden. [22]So the warden put Joseph in charge of all those held in the prison, and he was made responsible for all that was done there. [23]The warden paid no attention to anything under Joseph's care, because the Lord was with Joseph and gave him success in whatever he did.

Joseph remained in prison another two years because the cup bearer did not mention him to Pharaoh, yet he was still willing to interpret the dream without ill will toward the cupbearer. The secure base attached individual has a great capacity for forgiveness and resiliency

Genesis 40:23-41:1

The chief cupbearer, however, did not remember Joseph; he forgot him. [41:1]When two full years had passed, Pharaoh had a dream: He was standing by the Nile

Even though he married a woman who was not an Israelite, Joseph continued to worship because he had a secure base attachment that perpetuated his relationship

Genesis 41:50-51

Before the years of famine came, two sons were born to Joseph by Asenath daughter of Potiphera, priest of On. [51]Joseph named his firstborn Manasseh

with God.	and said, "It is because God has made me forget all my trouble and all my father's household."
Job continued to worship Yahweh. A secure base attached individual maintains his relationship with God regardless of his predicament.	**Job 1:13-22** One day when Job's sons and daughters were feasting and drinking wine at the oldest brother's house, [14]a messenger came to Job and said, "The oxen were plowing and the donkeys were grazing nearby, [15]and the Sabeans attacked and carried them off. They put the servants to the sword, and I am the only one who has escaped to tell you!" [16]While he was still speaking, another messenger came and said, "The fire of God fell from the sky and burned up the sheep and the servants, and I am the only one who has escaped to tell you!" [17]While he was still speaking, another messenger came and said, "The Chaldeans formed three raiding parties and swept down on your camels and carried them off. They put the servants to the sword, and I am the only one who has escaped to tell you!" [18]While he was still speaking, yet another messenger came and said, "Your sons and daughters were feasting and drinking wine at the oldest brother's house, [19]when suddenly a mighty wind swept in from the desert and struck the four corners of the house. It collapsed on them

and they are dead, and I am the only one who has escaped to tell you!" [20]At this, Job got up and tore his robe and shaved his head. Then he fell to the ground in worship [21]and said: "Naked I came from my mother's womb, and naked I will depart. The Lord gave and the Lord has taken away; may the name of the Lord be praised." [22]In all this, Job did not sin by charging God with wrongdoing.

Job 2:10

He replied, "You are talking like a foolish woman. Shall we accept good from God, and not trouble?" In all this, Job did not sin in what he said.

Job exemplifies secure base attachment by interceding for his friends. This is another example of how a person with secure base attachment has the capacity to forgive those who wrong him.

Job 42:1-8

Then Job replied to the Lord: [2]"I know that you can do all things; no plan of yours can be thwarted. [3]You asked, 'Who is this that obscures my counsel without knowledge?' Surely I spoke of things I did not understand, things too wonderful for me to know. [4]"You said, 'Listen now, and I will speak; I will question you, and you shall answer me.' [5]My ears had heard of you but now my eyes have seen you. [6]Therefore I despise myself and repent in dust and ashes." [7]After the Lord had said these things to Job, he said to Eliphaz the Temanite, "I am angry with you and your two friends, because you have not spoken of me what is right, as my servant Job has. [8]So now take seven bulls and seven rams and go to my servant Job and sacrifice a burnt offering for yourselves. My servant Job will pray for you, and I will accept his prayer and not deal with you according to your folly. You have not spoken of me what is right, as my servant Job has."

Psychospiritual resiliency emphasizes self-corrective behavior that leads to a constructive outcome. Re-parenting can help provide the strength to overcome adversity.

James 5:11

As you know, we consider blessed those who have persevered. You have heard of Job's perseverance and have seen what the Lord finally brought about. The Lord is full of compassion and mercy.

A significant number of believers, including those in full-time ministry, lose faith because they lack a secure base attachment and therefore have little spiritual resiliency. In Joshua 3:16-17, all Israel followed the ark of the Lord to provide protection. In the same manner, re-parenting offers protection until the person achieves spiritual maturity.

Joshua 6:13

The seven priests carrying the seven trumpets went forward, marching before the ark of the Lord and blowing the trumpets. The armed men went ahead of them and the rear guard followed the ark of the Lord, while the trumpets kept sounding.

Isaiah 52:12

But you will not leave in haste or go in flight; for the Lord will

	go before you, the God of Israel will be your rear guard. Isaiah 58:8 Then your light will break forth like the dawn, and your healing will quickly appear; then your righteousness will go before you, and the glory of the Lord will be your rear guard.

Worship strengthens love for the Father. Love compels people to establish a relationship with those who are in bondage. An intimate relationship with God enables believers to rejoice in their faith and accomplish much because they have a holy connection to the Almighty. The greater the intensity of worship, the greater the capacity for compassion, mercy, and empathy. The strong relationship with God born from worship allows the establishment of a long-term commitment that will transform the church. Nehemiah was a man of prayer, and that gift translated into compassion for the Israelites.

Nehemiah 1:4

When I heard these things, I sat down and wept. For some days I mourned and fasted and prayed before the God of heaven.

Nehemiah 1:6

Let your ear be attentive and your eyes open to hear the prayer your servant is praying before you day and night for your servants, the people of Israel. I confess the sins we Israelites, including myself and my father's house, have committed against you.

Worshiping enhances the Father-child (vertical) relationship and helps believers cultivate the courage needed to move from stagnation, to action, and then transformation. Paul wrote, "Be transformed by the renewing of your mind" (Rom. 12:2). Transforming belief systems means being *transfigured.* The word metamorphosis (from the Greek word *metamophoo*) means "to change in character or condition."[12]

People with secure base attachment form close-bonded relationships that provide a sense of safety and protection. When such a relationship is hindered or threatened, they instinctively react by moving closer to God through prayer, as seen in the lives of Job and Joseph. Prayer in turn gives believers the ability to forgive, and forgiveness preserves their relationships.

Adoring and praising God are forms of secure base attachment style. Job and Joseph were excellent examples of this concept as they nurtured their secure base attachment with God through adoration and worship. Worship gave them the strength to overcome adversity.

Ephesians 6:12

For our struggle is not against flesh and blood, but against the rulers, against the authorities, against the powers of this dark world and against the spiritual forces of evil in the heavenly realms.

2 Corinthians 10:3-4

For though we live in the world, we do not wage war as the world does. [4]The weapons we fight with are not the weapons of the world. On the contrary, they have divine power to demolish strongholds.

---

12 S. Zodhiates, *The Complete Word Study Dictionary New Testament* (Chattanooga, TN: AMG International, Inc, 1993).

Without a secure base attachment, people who are involved in spiritual warfare become ineffective because they lack the psychological, emotional, and spiritual support systems that will help them survive troubled times. Individuals with avoidant attachment are especially vulnerable to negative influences.

Chapter 3

Spiritual Consequences:
Anxious Ambivalent Attachment

People with an anxious ambivalent attachment often find it difficult to function in a group setting. If the ambivalent disorder is mild, they may form short-term group support systems, but such relationships usually do not last long. These people are insecure and hypersensitive to feedback, making it difficult to acquire insight into their own responsibility within relationships. As adults, most anxious ambivalent people still have not resolved the inconsistent and intermittent parenting they received—they are riddled with negative emotions such as anger and hurt. These emotions create psychospiritual liabilities such as immaturity, passivity, dependency, and low frustration tolerance. In turn, they are unable to commit to long-term reciprocal nurturing relationships, causing them to drift from one relationship—or one church—to another.

In their jobs, individuals with anxious ambivalent attachment will focus on the work that does not deal with personal relationships. When personnel conflicts arise they will attempt to remain in the background until the conflict is resolved. They may be able to provide some advice but there will be no mercy, compassion, or empathy. Criticism is personalized and instead of taking responsibility for their actions they will blame circumstances or other people.

David's Sons as Examples of Anxious Ambivalent Attachment

Adonijah, David's son, demonstrates anxious ambivalent attachment, which is documented by David's behavior to him. David never interfered with Adonijah. Therefore, as a parent, David perpetuated his son's anxious ambivalent attachment. Individuals who fall into a category other than secure base attachment are highly capable of premeditated immoral acts.	1 Kings 1:5-6 Now Adonijah, whose mother was Haggith, put himself forward and said, "I will be king." So he got chariots and horses ready, with fifty men to run ahead of him. ⁶(His father had never interfered with him by asking, "Why do you behave as you do?" He was also very handsome and was born next after Absalom.)
Adonijah wanted authority and got it by superficially developing relationships. Anxious ambivalent attachment individuals tend to be profoundly insecure and therefore need to be in control.	1 Kings 1:7-11 Adonijah conferred with Joab son of Zeruiah and with Abiathar the priest, and they gave him their support. ⁸But Zadok the priest, Benaiah son of Jehoiada, Nathan the prophet, Shimei and Rei and David's special guard did not join Adonijah. ⁹Adonijah then sacrificed sheep, cattle and fattened calves at the Stone of Zoheleth near En Rogel. He invited all his brothers, the king's sons, and all the men of Judah who were royal officials, ¹⁰but he did not invite Nathan the prophet or Benaiah or the special guard or his brother Solomon. ¹¹Then Nathan asked Bathsheba, Solomon's mother,

David's son Amnon, raped his half sister Tamar. It was premeditated. This is an example of attachment disorder behavior from a psychospiritual standpoint. It also demonstrates the impact of generational sin, an example of which is David's sexual sin with Bathsheba which he passed on to his son Amnon. Amnon listened to Jonadab. Jonadab was Amnon's cousin. His father, Shimeah, was the third born of the seven sons of Jesse. It is possible that Shimeah felt overlooked when Samuel did not choose him. Shimeah, also known as Shammah, served under Saul. His oldest brother was not pleased to see David and did not think well of him, it is possible that Shemeah felt the same way.

Parents need to be vigilant of family relationships with the children that need re-

"Have you not heard that Adonijah, the son of Haggith, has become king without our lord David's knowing it?

1 Samuel 16:9
Jesse then had Shammah pass by, but Samuel said, "Nor has the Lord chosen this one."

1 Samuel 17:13
Jesse's three oldest sons had followed Saul to the war: The firstborn was Eliab; the second, Abinadab; and the third, Shammah.

1 Chronicles 2:13
Jesse was the father of Eliab his firstborn; the second son was Abinadab, the third Shimea

1 Samuel 17:28
When Eliab, David's oldest brother, heard him speaking with the men, he burned with anger at him and asked, "Why have you come down here? And with whom did you leave those few sheep in the desert? I know how conceited you are and how wicked your heart is; you came down only to watch the battle."

2 Samuel 13:3-7
Now Amnon had a friend named Jonadab son of Shimeah,

parenting, as they are more vulnerable. David should have been more aware of not only Amnon's obsession with Tamar but with his relationship with his cousin whom the Bible describes as a shrewd man.

David's brother. Jonadab was a very shrewd man. ⁴He asked Amnon, "Why do you, the king's son, look so haggard morning after morning? Won't you tell me?" Amnon said to him, "I'm in love with Tamar, my brother Absalom's sister." ⁵"Go to bed and pretend to be ill," Jonadab said. "When your father comes to see you, say to him, 'I would like my sister Tamar to come and give me something to eat. Let her prepare the food in my sight so I may watch her and then eat it from her hand.' ⁶"So Amnon lay down and pretended to be ill. When the king came to see him, Amnon said to him, "I would like my sister Tamar to come and make some special bread in my sight, so I may eat from her hand." ⁷David sent word to Tamar at the palace: "Go to the house of your brother Amnon and prepare some food for him."

2 Samuel 13:10
Then Amnon said to Tamar, "Bring the food here into my bedroom so I may eat from your hand." And Tamar took the bread she had prepared and brought it to her brother Amnon in his bedroom.

	2 Samuel 13:13-14 What about me? Where could I get rid of my disgrace? And what about you? You would be like one of the wicked fools in Israel. Please speak to the king; he will not keep me from being married to you." [14]But he refused to listen to her, and since he was stronger than she, he raped her.
David mourned for Amnon even though he was furious that Amnon had raped Tamar. At times a parent's love for children minimizes the child's criminal behavior, thus, perpetuating generational sin.	**2 Samuel 13:21** When King David heard all this, he was furious.
David was still not discerning Jonadab's involvement in the death of Amnon.	**2 Samuel 13:32** But Jonadab son of Shimeah, David's brother, said, "My lord should not think that they killed all the princes; only Amnon is dead. This has been Absalom's expressed intention ever since the day Amnon raped his sister Tamar.
	2 Samuel 13:37-38 Absalom fled and went to Talmai son of Ammihud, the king of Geshur. But King David mourned for his son every day. [38] After Absalom fled and went to Geshur, he stayed there three years.

Absalom is also an example of anxious ambivalent attachment disorder. Absalom did not talk to Amnon for two years and then killed him. This type of personality is prone to narcissistic injury and can be highly vengeful. Absalom named his daughter after his sister Tamar, possibly as a way of justifying his act of vengeance toward Amnon. This in turn was a perpetuation of generational sin. An example is David's sin of killing Uriah, the husband of Bathsheba (2 Sam. 11). Absalom did not think he did anything wrong by killing Amnon because of Amnon's sin.

David was not aware of his sons' actions because there was no communication.

2 Samuel 13:22-23

Absalom never said a word to Amnon, either good or bad; he hated Amnon because he had disgraced his sister Tamar. [23]Two years later, when Absalom's sheepshearers were at Baal Hazor near the border of Ephraim, he invited all the king's sons to come there.

2 Samuel 14:27

Three sons and a daughter were born to Absalom. The daughter's name was Tamar, and she became a beautiful woman.

2 Samuel 14:32

Absalom said to Joab, "Look, I sent word to you and said, 'Come here so I can send you to the king to ask, "Why have I come from Geshur? It would be better for me if I were still there!" 'Now then, I want to see the king's face, and if I am guilty of anything, let him put me to death."

2 Samuel 13:32

But Jonadab son of Shimeah, David's brother, said, "My lord should not think that they killed all the princes; only Amnon is dead. This has been Absalom's expressed intention ever since

	the day Amnon raped his sister Tamar.
Absalom felt he was worthy of a monument. This is a concrete illustration of a need to be admired brought on by insecurity.	**2 Samuel 18:18** During his lifetime Absalom had taken a pillar and erected it in the King's Valley as a monument to himself, for he thought, "I have no son to carry on the memory of my name." He named the pillar after himself, and it is called Absalom's Monument to this day.
Absalom, Amnon, and Tamar did not have a relationship with each other. If we do not develop a healthy attachment with our parents, it is difficult to form close relationships with our siblings.	**2 Samuel 13:20** Her brother Absalom said to her, "Has that Amnon, your brother, been with you? Be quiet now, my sister; he is your brother. Don't take this thing to heart." And Tamar lived in her brother Absalom's house, a desolate woman. **2 Samuel 13:22** Absalom never said a word to Amnon, either good or bad; he hated Amnon because he had disgraced his sister Tamar.
Absalom's purpose in seeing David was to undermine David's authority. His reconciliation was not real; it only served his own desires of taking over David's throne.	**2 Samuel 15:1-6** In the course of time, Absalom provided himself with a chariot and horses and with fifty men to run ahead of him. ²He would get up early and stand by the

side of the road leading to the city gate. Whenever anyone came with a complaint to be placed before the king for a decision, Absalom would call out to him, "What town are you from?" He would answer, "Your servant is from one of the tribes of Israel." [3]Then Absalom would say to him, "Look, your claims are valid and proper, but there is no representative of the king to hear you." [4]And Absalom would add, "If only I were appointed judge in the land! Then everyone who has a complaint or case could come to me and I would see that he gets justice." [5]Also, whenever anyone approached him to bow down before him, Absalom would reach out his hand, take hold of him and kiss him. [6]Absalom behaved in this way toward all the Israelites who came to the king asking for justice, and so he stole the hearts of the men of Israel.

Absalom was a smooth talker; he needed people to need him, which reflects the typical insecurity of individuals with this attachment style.

2 Samuel 15:5-6

Also, whenever anyone approached him to bow down before him, Absalom would reach out his hand, take hold of him and kiss him. [6]Absalom behaved in this way toward all the Israelites who came to the king asking for justice, and so he stole the hearts of the men of Israel.

Absalom had the patience to work out long term plans. First he waited two years before killing Amnon, then another three years before trying to approach David. He spent four years sitting at the gate. People with this type of attachment are persistent when it is to their benefit.

2 Samuel 15:7-10
At the end of four years, Absalom said to the king, "Let me go to Hebron and fulfill a vow I made to the Lord. [8]While your servant was living at Geshur in Aram, I made this vow: 'If the Lord takes me back to Jerusalem, I will worship the Lord in Hebron.'" [9]The king said to him, "Go in peace." So he went to Hebron. [10]Then Absalom sent secret messengers throughout the tribes of Israel to say, "As soon as you hear the sound of the trumpets, then say, 'Absalom is king in Hebron.'"

Absalom offered sacrifices. This type of behavior can be classified as a form of political maneuvering to gain support and acceptance.

2 Samuel 15:11-13
Two hundred men from Jerusalem had accompanied Absalom. They had been invited as guests and went quite innocently, knowing nothing about the matter. [12]While Absalom was offering sacrifices, he also sent for Ahithophel the Gilonite, David's counselor, to come from Giloh, his hometown. And so the conspiracy gained strength, and Absalom's following kept on increasing. [13]A messenger came and told

David once again did not confront his son. Lax parenting discipline tends to reinforce incorrigible behavior.

Absalom was unable to even trust someone he and his father knew inquired of God. So Absalom questioned his father's friend. This type of attachment individual is unable to trust anyone, even when he knows the person is trustworthy. This lack of trust has nothing to do with the trustworthiness of others.

Absalom hears what he wants to hear and rationalizes the rest. Because of their insecurity and inadequacy, people with this type of

David, "The hearts of the men of Israel are with Absalom."

2 Samuel 15:14
Then David said to all his officials who were with him in Jerusalem, "Come! We must flee, or none of us will escape from Absalom. We must leave immediately, or he will move quickly to overtake us and bring ruin upon us and put the city to the sword."

2 Samuel 16:23
Now in those days the advice Ahithophel gave was like that of one who inquires of God. That was how both David and Absalom regarded all of Ahithophel's advice.

2 Samuel 17:5-6
But Absalom said, "Summon also Hushai the Arkite, so we can hear what he has to say." ⁶When Hushai came to him, Absalom said, "Ahithophel has given this advice. Should we do what he says? If not, give us your opinion."

2 Samuel 17:11-14
"So I advise you: Let all Israel, from Dan to Beersheba—as numerous as the sand on the seashore—be gathered to you,

attachment style have brittle coping skills that prevent them from being teachable and receptive to rebuke.

with you yourself leading them into battle. [12]Then we will attack him wherever he may be found, and we will fall on him as dew settles on the ground. Neither he nor any of his men will be left alive. [13]If he withdraws into a city, then all Israel will bring ropes to that city, and we will drag it down to the valley until not even a piece of it can be found." [14]Absalom and all the men of Israel said, "The advice of Hushai the Arkite is better than that of Ahithophel." For the Lord had determined to frustrate the good advice of Ahithophel in order to bring disaster on Absalom.

David allowed Absalom to come back, but he did not restore the relationship. This is an indication that David did not foster a secure relationship with Absalom.

2 Samuel 14:21-24

The king said to Joab, "Very well, I will do it. Go, bring back the young man Absalom." [22]Joab fell with his face to the ground to pay him honor, and he blessed the king. Joab said, "Today your servant knows that he has found favor in your eyes, my lord the king, because the king has granted his servant's request." [23]Then Joab went to Geshur and brought Absalom back to Jerusalem. [24]But the king said, "He must go to his own house; he must not see my face." So Absalom went to his own house and did not see the face of the king.

David still was not ready to face up to disciplining his son.	2 Samuel 18:5 The king commanded Joab, Abishai and Ittai, "Be gentle with the young man Absalom for my sake." And all the troops heard the king giving orders concerning Absalom to each of the commanders.
David's concern was for his son, but he did not really have a relationship with him. Asking about Absalom's safety was probably due to his realization of failure in parenting Absalom rather than the desire to establish a secure base relationship.	2 Samuel 18:29 The king asked, "Is the young man Absalom safe?" Ahimaaz answered, "I saw great confusion just as Joab was about to send the king's servant and me, your servant, but I don't know what it was."
David's repentance is shown by his response to Absalom's death. Perhaps that's why he could parent Solomon in a more appropriate manner. Without repentance of an individual's sin the consequences of generational sin cannot be terminated.	2 Samuel 18:33 The king was shaken. He went up to the room over the gateway and wept. As he went, he said: "O my son Absalom! My son, my son Absalom! If only I had died instead of you—O Absalom, my son, my son!"
	2 Samuel 19:4-6 The king covered his face and cried aloud, "O my son Absalom! O Absalom, my son, my son!" ⁵Then Joab went into the house to the king and said, "Today you have humiliated all your men, who have just saved

	your life and the lives of your sons and daughters and the lives of your wives and concubines. [6]You love those who hate you and hate those who love you. You have made it clear today that the commanders and their men mean nothing to you. I see that you would be pleased if Absalom were alive today and all of us were dead.

Moses as an Example of Anxious Ambivalent Attachment

| Parenting was disrupted between Moses and his mother, resulting in anxious ambivalent attachment style for Moses. The purpose for abandonment was to save Moses' life, but in spite of this justification, abandonment produced the <u>same consequences—anxious ambivalent attachment. It is important to note that</u> even though someone may intellectually understand why they were given up for adoption, emotionally they will still have a sense of psychological abandonment. | Exodus 2:1-3 Now a man of the house of Levi married a Levite woman, [2]and she became pregnant and gave birth to a son. When she saw that he was a fine child, she hid him for three months. [3]But when she could hide him no longer, she got a papyrus basket for him and coated it with tar and pitch. Then she placed the child in it and put it among the reeds along the bank of the Nile. |
| Infants could have been nursed up to three years, so Moses had time to develop an attachment with his mother. | Exodus 2:4-10 His sister stood at a distance to see what would happen to him. [5]Then Pharaoh's daughter went |

The disruptions of this secure base attachment resulted in an anxious ambivalent relationship. When Moses' mother took him to Pharaoh's daughter, he lost all that was familiar to him; people, lifestyle, diet, name—in essence his identity. This caused him to grow up feeling insecure, inadequate, lacking self-worth and self-confidence. This is shown by his interaction with the great I AM during the burning bush incident in which he used the excuse of lacking eloquent speech (Exod. 4:10).

Moses was aware that he did not belong with his own people. He knew the differences between his lifestyle and position and theirs. He wanted to be part of his people. He wanted to be a leader, but did not know how. Like Moses, the anxious ambivalent person craves a secure base relationship.

down to the Nile to bathe, and her attendants were walking along the river bank. She saw the basket among the reeds and sent her slave girl to get it. [6]She opened it and saw the baby. He was crying, and she felt sorry for him. "This is one of the Hebrew babies," she said. [7]Then his sister asked Pharaoh's daughter, "Shall I go and get one of the Hebrew women to nurse the baby for you?" [8]"Yes, go," she answered. And the girl went and got the baby's mother. [9]Pharaoh's daughter said to her, "Take this baby and nurse him for me, and I will pay you." So the woman took the baby and nursed him. [10]When the child grew older, she took him to Pharaoh's daughter and he became her son. She named him Moses, saying, "I drew him out of the water."

Exodus 2:11-14

One day, after Moses had grown up, he went out to where his own people were and watched them at their hard labor. He saw an Egyptian beating a Hebrew, one of his own people. [12]Glancing this way and that and seeing no one, he killed the Egyptian and hid him in the sand. [13]The next day he went out and saw two Hebrews fighting. He asked the

	one in the wrong, "Why are you hitting your fellow Hebrew?" [14]The man said, "Who made you ruler and judge over us? Are you thinking of killing me as you killed the Egyptian?" Then Moses was afraid and thought, "What I did must have become known."
Moses was not secure in his relationship with Pharaoh, even though Pharaoh was his adopted grandfather.	Exodus 2:14b-15 Then Moses was afraid and thought, "What I did must have become known." When Pharaoh heard of this, he tried to kill Moses, but Moses fled from Pharaoh and went to live in Midian, where he sat down by a well.
Moses did know the right thing to do. These types of attachment individuals do have the capacity for self awareness and psychological insight. Unfortunately, they do not have the understanding or psychospiritual knowledge to establish a secure base attachment on their own.	Exodus 2:17 Some shepherds came along and drove them away, but Moses got up and came to their rescue and watered their flock.
Moses must have felt like an alien in his homeland as well as in Midian. The sense of belonging is not geographical, but psychospiritual.	Exodus 2:21-22 Moses agreed to stay with the man, who gave his daughter Zipporah to Moses in marriage. [22]Zipporah gave birth to a son, and Moses named him Gershom, saying, "I have

become an alien in a foreign land."

Moses' insecurity is evident here. Even though he was raised in Pharaoh's home, had a wife and child, an occupation, and was accepted into his father-in-law's house, he still did not believe in his own potential. The leadership he tried to exhibit when he killed the Egyptian does not appear so attractive when he must be accountable to God.

Exodus 3:11-13

But Moses said to God, "Who am I, that I should go to Pharaoh and bring the Israelites out of Egypt?" [12]And God said, "I will be with you. And this will be the sign to you that it is I who have sent you: When you have brought the people out of Egypt, you will worship God on this mountain." [13]Moses said to God, "Suppose I go to the Israelites and say to them, 'The God of your fathers has sent me to you,' and they ask me, 'What is his name?' Then what shall I tell them?"

God gave Moses specifics, but Moses still did not want to go due to his lack of self-confidence. His insecurity showed itself as lack of confidence in God.

Exodus 3:14-22

God said to Moses, "I am who I am. This is what you are to say to the Israelites: 'I am has sent me to you.'" [15]God also said to Moses, "Say to the Israelites, 'The Lord, the God of your fathers—the God of Abraham, the God of Isaac and the God of Jacob—has sent me to you.' This is my name forever, the name by which I am to be remembered from generation to generation. [16]"Go, assemble the elders of Israel and say to them, 'The Lord, the God of your fathers—the God of

Abraham, Isaac and Jacob—
appeared to me and said: I
have watched over you and
have seen what has been done
to you in Egypt. [17]And I have
promised to bring you up out of
your misery in Egypt into the
land of the Canaanites, Hittites,
Amorites, Perizzites, Hivites
and Jebusites—a land flowing
with milk and honey.' [18]"The
elders of Israel will listen to
you. Then you and the elders
are to go to the king of Egypt
and say to him, 'The Lord, the
God of the Hebrews, has met
with us. Let us take a three-day
journey into the desert to offer
sacrifices to the Lord our God.'
[19]But I know that the king of
Egypt will not let you go unless
a mighty hand compels him.
[20]So I will stretch out my hand
and strike the Egyptians with all
the wonders that I will perform
among them. After that, he
will let you go. [21]"And I will
make the Egyptians favorably
disposed toward this people,
so that when you leave you will
not go empty-handed. [22]Every
woman is to ask her neighbor
and any woman living in her
house for articles of silver and
gold and for clothing, which
you will put on your sons and
daughters. And so you will
plunder the Egyptians."

Moses kept questioning God, but he did not really want answers—he just did not want to be responsible. This is a good illustration of someone who rationalizes the fear of responsibility by having anticipatory anxiety.

Exodus 4:1

Moses answered, "What if they do not believe me or listen to me and say, 'The Lord did not appear to you'?"

Exodus 4:8-9

Then the Lord said, "If they do not believe you or pay attention to the first miraculous sign, they may believe the second. ⁹But if they do not believe these two signs or listen to you, take some water from the Nile and pour it on the dry ground. The water you take from the river will become blood on the ground."

God allowed Aaron to help Moses, but still required Moses to do his part. Moses had to speak everything God told him to Aaron. Moses used his excuse of stuttering to not obey God and never asked for healing in spite of God's awesome manifestation of power. Due to insecurity, this type of person tends to use his personal shortcomings as justification not to be used by God. No matter how many times they receive prayer for healing they are unable to appropriate it because it will remove their reason for not being able to do some tasks.

Exodus 4:10-17

Moses said to the Lord, "O Lord, I have never been eloquent, neither in the past nor since you have spoken to your servant. I am slow of speech and tongue." ¹¹The Lord said to him, "Who gave man his mouth? Who makes him deaf or mute? Who gives him sight or makes him blind? Is it not I, the Lord? ¹²Now go; I will help you speak and will teach you what to say." ¹³But Moses said, "O Lord, please send someone else to do it." ¹⁴Then the Lord's anger burned against Moses and he said, "What about your brother, Aaron the Levite? I know he can speak well. He is already on his way to meet you, and his heart will be glad when he sees you. ¹⁵You shall speak to him and put words in his mouth; I will help both of you speak and will teach you what to do. ¹⁶He will speak to the people for you, and it will be as if he were your mouth and as if you were God to him. ¹⁷But take this staff in your hand so you can perform miraculous signs with it."

Exodus 7:2
You are to say everything I command you, and your brother Aaron is to tell Pharaoh to let the Israelites go out of his country.

Moses may have been hoping his father-in-law would not give him permission to go. This would further justify his lack of worthiness to be used of God.

Exodus 4:18
Then Moses went back to Jethro his father-in-law and said to him, "Let me go back to my own people in Egypt to see if any of them are still alive." Jethro said, "Go, and I wish you well."

Even though Miriam was a prophetess, she and Moses had difficulties and did not have a healthy relationship. Their problems were not caused by major spiritual issues, but by

Exodus 15:20
Then Miriam the prophetess, Aaron's sister, took a tambourine in her hand, and all the women followed her, with tambourines and dancing.

personal issues. Believers with anxious ambivalent attachment style can agree about spiritual issues, but get caught up with day to day issues. Miriam was the oldest; Aaron was three years older than Moses. Miriam and Aaron witnessed Moses being given away by their mother. This could then increase anticipatory anxiety and insecurity due to the uncertainty of family stability. Anticipatory anxiety causes feelings of "Will this happen to me?" that would create separation anxiety among the siblings as well as a sense of guilt. Even though they were prophets, they still struggled with insecurity caused by their family history.

During the plague, Moses was in constant communication with God and seemed to be obedient. Remember, God had already told him everything that would happen up to that point. When the Israelites were afraid as they camped, Moses had the right thing to say, but did not really know what God wanted him to do. God expected him to know. It is possible God had already told Moses what to do, as He had during all the other steps

Numbers 12:1

Miriam and Aaron began to talk against Moses because of his Cushite wife, for he had married a Cushite.

Exodus 7:1

Then the Lord said to Moses, "See, I have made you like God to Pharaoh, and your brother Aaron will be your prophet.

Exodus 7:7

Moses was eighty years old and Aaron eighty-three when they spoke to Pharaoh.

Exodus 14:9-15

The Egyptians—all Pharaoh's horses and chariots, horsemen and troops—pursued the Israelites and overtook them as they camped by the sea near Pi Hahiroth, opposite Baal Zephon. [10]As Pharaoh approached, the Israelites looked up, and there were the Egyptians, marching after them. They were terrified and cried out to the Lord. [11]They said to Moses, "Was it because there were no graves in Egypt

Moses was to take. But lack of self-confidence that eventually infected his confidence in God may have kept Moses from remembering what God had already told him. Stress affects memory due to neurodeterioration.

that you brought us to the desert to die? What have you done to us by bringing us out of Egypt? [12]Didn't we say to you in Egypt, 'Leave us alone; let us serve the Egyptians'? It would have been better for us to serve the Egyptians than to die in the desert!" [13]Moses answered the people, "Do not be afraid. Stand firm and you will see the deliverance the Lord will bring you today. The Egyptians you see today you will never see again. [14]The Lord will fight for you; you need only to be still." [15]Then the Lord said to Moses, "Why are you crying out to me? Tell the Israelites to move on.

Moses had a sense of anticipatory anxiety about continuing his task from God, because he did not have the people's support. Anxious ambivalent people need constant emotional support and nurturing. Without it, they tend to revert back to their sense of insecurity and self-doubt.

Exodus 15:24

So the people grumbled against Moses, saying, "What are we to drink?"

Exodus 16:2

In the desert the whole community grumbled against Moses and Aaron.

Exodus 16:20

However, some of them paid no attention to Moses; they kept part of it until morning, but it was full of maggots and began to smell. So Moses was angry with them.

	Exodus 16:27 Nevertheless, some of the people went out on the seventh day to gather it, but they found none. Exodus 17:2-4 So they quarreled with Moses and said, "Give us water to drink." Moses replied, "Why do you quarrel with me? Why do you put the Lord to the test?" ³But the people were thirsty for water there, and they grumbled against Moses. They said, "Why did you bring us up out of Egypt to make us and our children and livestock die of thirst?" ⁴Then Moses cried out to the Lord, "What am I to do with these people? They are almost ready to stone me."
Moses needed to be needed. He did not appear to be worried about his stuttering because he had a place of authority that was recognizable by the world; unlike the authority God gave him for the exodus which was not recognizable by the world. Anxious ambivalent individuals need affirmation by the world.	Exodus 18:13-16 The next day Moses took his seat to serve as judge for the people, and they stood around him from morning till evening. ¹⁴When his father-in-law saw all that Moses was doing for the people, he said, "What is this you are doing for the people? Why do you alone sit as judge, while all these people stand around you from morning till evening?" ¹⁵Moses answered him, "Because the people come to me to seek God's will.

Moses needed someone to make decisions for him in order to deflect any consequences or ramifications of his decision, again this is a reflection of his insecurity even though he has the delegated authority from God.

¹⁶"Whenever they have a dispute, it is brought to me, and I decide between the parties and inform them of God's decrees and laws."

Exodus 18:24
Moses listened to his father-in-law and did everything he said.

Numbers 9:1
The Lord spoke to Moses in the Desert of Sinai in the first month of the second year after they came out of Egypt. He said,

Numbers 10:29-31
Now Moses said to Hobab son of Reuel the Midianite, Moses' father-in-law, "We are setting out for the place about which the Lord said, 'I will give it to you.' Come with us and we will treat you well, for the Lord has promised good things to Israel." ³⁰He answered, "No, I will not go; I am going back to my own land and my own people." ³¹But Moses said, "Please do not leave us. You know where we should camp in the desert, and you can be our eyes.

Moses was an intermediary between God and the Israelites

Exodus 24:7-8
Then he took the Book of the

out of obedience to God. The anxious ambivalent type is highly capable of being obedient but without being re-parented their ability for compassion and mercy is still highly limited.

Moses learned to intercede for the Israelites out of respect to God, but still at this point it can be speculated that Moses had not established a relationship with the Israelites on a personal basis.

Covenant and read it to the people. They responded, "We will do everything the Lord has said; we will obey." [8]Moses then took the blood, sprinkled it on the people and said, "This is the blood of the covenant that the Lord has made with you in accordance with all these words."

Exodus 32:10-14

Now leave me alone so that my anger may burn against them and that I may destroy them. Then I will make you into a great nation." [11]But Moses sought the favor of the Lord his God. "O Lord," he said, "why should your anger burn against your people, whom you brought out of Egypt with great power and a mighty hand? [12]Why should the Egyptians say, 'It was with evil intent that he brought them out, to kill them in the mountains and to wipe them off the face of the earth'? Turn from your fierce anger; relent and do not bring disaster on your people. [13]Remember your servants Abraham, Isaac and Israel, to whom you swore by your own self: 'I will make your descendants as numerous as the stars in the sky and I will give your descendants all this land I promised them, and it will be their inheritance forever.'" [14]Then the Lord relented and did not bring on his people the disaster he had threatened.

Exodus 32:31-32

So Moses went back to the Lord and said, "Oh, what a great sin these people have committed! They have made themselves gods of gold. [32]But now, please forgive their sin—but if not, then blot me out of the book you have written."

Moses finally asked God to teach him. The simplest solutions can be found by just asking God. At this juncture it is plausible that Moses recognized that he is a leader out of respect to God but that he lacks mercy and compassion for God's people.

Exodus 33:11-13

The Lord would speak to Moses face to face, as a man speaks with his friend. Then Moses would return to the camp, but his young aide Joshua son of Nun did not leave the tent. [12]Moses said to the Lord, "You have been telling me, 'Lead these people,' but you have not let me know whom you will send with me. You have said, 'I know you by name and you have found favor with me.' [13]If you are pleased with me, teach me your ways so I may know you and continue to find favor with you. Remember that this nation is your people."

Moses asked God to be with them. Anxious ambivalent people are fearful of dependency on anyone for fear of abandonment. At this juncture of Moses' relationship and interaction with God, it appears he is beginning to establish a dependency on God.

Exodus 33:15-16

Then Moses said to him, "If your Presence does not go with us, do not send us up from here. ¹⁶How will anyone know that you are pleased with me and with your people unless you go with us? What else will distinguish me and your people from all the other people on the face of the earth?"

Exodus 33:17

And the Lord said to Moses, "I will do the very thing you have asked, because I am pleased with you and I know you by name."

Moses went from frustration with the Israelites, for little things like keeping the manna until morning, to interceding for them for the golden calf, to blessing them. Moses now is able to be consistent in his love and compassion for God's people but only after his sense of dependency on God became reality. Once the anxious ambivalent individual establishes a reciprocal relationship, then love and mercy become possible as the agent of God to others.

Exodus 16:20

However, some of them paid no attention to Moses; they kept part of it until morning, but it was full of maggots and began to smell. So Moses was angry with them.

Exodus 16:28

Then the Lord said to Moses, "How long will you refuse to keep my commands and my instructions?

Exodus 17:2

So they quarreled with Moses and said, "Give us water to drink." Moses replied, "Why

	do you quarrel with me? Why do you put the Lord to the test?"
	Exodus 17:4
	Then Moses cried out to the Lord, "What am I to do with these people? They are almost ready to stone me."
	Exodus 39:43
	Moses inspected the work and saw that they had done it just as the Lord had commanded. So Moses blessed them.
	Deuteronomy 33:1
	This is the blessing that Moses the man of God pronounced on the Israelites before his death.
Moses reproduced himself by preparing Joshua as a replacement. In essence, Moses was re-parenting Joshua. As a parent he wanted the child to exceed and be successful far beyond his own accomplishments. As this point in Moses' life his anxious ambivalent attachment was diminishing and being transformed into a more secure base relationship with God and eventually to His people by being able to exercise identification repentance on their behalf.	Exodus 17:9
	Moses said to Joshua, "Choose some of our men and go out to fight the Amalekites. Tomorrow I will stand on top of the hill with the staff of God in my hands."
	Deuteronomy 31:7
	Then Moses summoned Joshua and said to him in the presence of all Israel, "Be strong and courageous, for you must go with this people into the land that the Lord swore to their

Moses instructed Joshua. Now that Moses had developed a secure base attachment, procedurally the generational sin (the murder of the Egyptian, Exod. 2:11-12) was transformed to generational blessing.

forefathers to give them, and you must divide it among them as their inheritance.

Exodus 17:14
Then the Lord said to Moses, "Write this on a scroll as something to be remembered and make sure that Joshua hears it, because I will completely blot out the memory of Amalek from under heaven."

Exodus 24:13
Then Moses set out with Joshua his aide, and Moses went up on the mountain of God.

Exodus 32:17
When Joshua heard the noise of the people shouting, he said to Moses, "There is the sound of war in the camp."

Exodus 33:11
The Lord would speak to Moses face to face, as a man speaks with his friend. Then Moses would return to the camp, but his young aide Joshua son of Nun did not leave the tent.

Numbers 11:28
Joshua son of Nun, who had been Moses' aide since youth, spoke up and said, "Moses, my lord, stop them!"

Moses publicly recognized Joshua as his replacement. Only individuals with a secure base attachment are able to relinquish authority.	**Numbers 27:18-22** So the Lord said to Moses, "Take Joshua son of Nun, a man in whom is the spirit, and lay your hand on him. ¹⁹Have him stand before Eleazar the priest and the entire assembly and commission him in their presence. ²⁰Give him some of your authority so the whole Israelite community will obey him. ²¹He is to stand before Eleazar the priest, who will obtain decisions for him by inquiring of the Urim before the Lord. At his command he and the entire community of the Israelites will go out, and at his command they will come in." ²²Moses did as the Lord commanded him. He took Joshua and had him stand before Eleazar the priest and the whole assembly. **Deuteronomy 3:28** But commission Joshua, and encourage and strengthen him, for he will lead this people across and will cause them to inherit the land that you will see." **Deuteronomy 31:7** Then Moses summoned Joshua and said to him in the presence of all Israel, "Be strong and courageous, for you must go

	with this people into the land that the Lord swore to their forefathers to give them, and you must divide it among them as their inheritance.
Moses laid hands on Joshua to set him apart as his successor.	Deuteronomy 34:9 Now Joshua son of Nun was filled with the spirit of wisdom because Moses had laid his hands on him. So the Israelites listened to him and did what the Lord had commanded Moses.
Moses finished strong. This is an indication of God's grace and mercy upon Moses by granting him inner healing of his anxious ambivalent attachment. He was transformed and therefore able to have a secure base attachment relationship both with God and His people.	Deuteronomy 34:7 Moses was a hundred and twenty years old when he died, yet his eyes were not weak nor his strength gone.
Aaron had anxious ambivalent attachment. Even though Aaron was older, and not the child given away, he had difficulty with his relationship with Moses and thought he should be on equal ground. He may have envied Moses' privileged upbringing. Regardless of the level of severity of the break in parenting, it still affects the child.	Exodus 7:7 Moses was eighty years old and Aaron eighty-three when they spoke to Pharaoh. Numbers 12:1-2 Miriam and Aaron began to talk against Moses because of his Cushite wife, for he had married a Cushite. ²"Has the Lord spoken only through Moses?" they asked. "Hasn't

When Aaron's time came to be in charge, he faltered by trying to mix worshiping the Lord and worshiping the golden calf, and then did not take responsibility for his actions. Just like Moses, Aaron showed insecurity that compelled him to bolster his sense of self-confidence by trying to please everyone rather than taking the risk of being rejected by anyone. Insecure individuals tend to succumb to the demands and pressure of the situation and justify their behavior by projecting their responsibilities onto others for their actions.

he also spoken through us?" And the Lord heard this.

Exodus 32:1-5

When the people saw that Moses was so long in coming down from the mountain, they gathered around Aaron and said, "Come, make us gods who will go before us. As for this fellow Moses who brought us up out of Egypt, we don't know what has happened to him." [2]Aaron answered them, "Take off the gold earrings that your wives, your sons and your daughters are wearing, and bring them to me." [3]So all the people took off their earrings and brought them to Aaron. [4]He took what they handed him and made it into an idol cast in the shape of a calf, fashioning it with a tool. Then they said, "These are your gods, O Israel, who brought you up out of Egypt." [5]When Aaron saw this, he built an altar in front of the calf and announced, "Tomorrow there will be a festival to the Lord."

Exodus 32:21-24

He said to Aaron, "What did these people do to you, that you led them into such great sin?" [22]"Do not be angry, my lord," Aaron answered. "You know how prone these people are to

	evil. [23]They said to me, 'Make us gods who will go before us. As for this fellow Moses who brought us up out of Egypt, we don't know what has happened to him.' [24]So I told them, 'Whoever has any gold jewelry, take it off.' Then they gave me the gold, and I threw it into the fire, and out came this calf!"

Chapter 4

Spiritual Consequences:
Avoidant Attachment

People who have an avoidant attachment style struggle with hypersensitivity, inhibition, devaluation of self, and a chronic sense of emptiness. They seek privacy as a self-protective measure; in addition, they have egocentric and narcissistic tendencies.

People with avoidant attachment live with a sense of entitlement that springs from their pervasive feelings of emotional deprivation and neglect. This sense of entitlement makes it difficult for them to sustain relationships.

Saul As An Example Of Avoidant Attachment

Saul came from a rich, influential family; however, socioeconomic environment has no direct bearing on the type of attachment style an individual inherits from his or her parents.	1 Samuel 9:1 There was a Benjamite, a man of standing, whose name was Kish son of Abiel, the son of Zeror, the son of Becorath, the son of Aphiah of Benjamin.
Saul was the most handsome man in Israel, head and shoulders taller than anyone else in the land. Positive physical attributes do not guarantee a secure base attachment.	1 Samuel 9:2 He had a son named Saul, an impressive young man without equal among the Israelite—a head taller than any of the others.

When they couldn't find the donkeys, Saul was ready to go home. Evidently he was rich enough that the loss of donkeys did not trouble him. Avoidant attachment style individuals tend to base their self-confidence upon their economic status.

1 Samuel 9:5
When they reached the district of Zuph, Saul said to the servant who was with him, "Come, let's go back, or my father will stop thinking about the donkeys and start worrying about us."

Saul thought he needed money to get advice from a man of God. Maybe he was not used to getting help or offering help without an exchange of goods or services. This type of attachment style has profound difficulty with the concept of being emotionally indebted.

1 Samuel 9:6-7
But the servant replied, "Look, in this town there is a man of God; he is highly respected, and everything he says comes true. Let's go there now. Perhaps he will tell us what way to take." [7]Saul said to his servant, "If we go, what can we give the man? The food in our sacks is gone. We have no gift to take to the man of God. What do we have?"

Saul did not hesitate to accept the offer of his servant's money. When an avoidant attachment individual does establish a relationship it tends to take the form of a codependency relationship.

1 Samuel 9:8
The servant answered him again. "Look," he said, "I have a quarter of a shekel of silver. I will give it to the man of God so that he will tell us what way to take."

1 Samuel 9:10
"Good," Saul said to his servant. "Come, let's go." So they set out for the town where the man of God was.

Samuel told Saul that the Spirit of the Lord would come upon him with power and that he would prophesy with a band of prophets and become a new person. He was, according to Samuel, to do whatever he thought best because God was with him. Saul was probably able to prophesy because he was under the covering of the other prophets. Avoidant personalities are highly susceptible to the influence of group process. In spite of Saul's avoidant attachment style, God used supernatural spiritual empowerment to demonstrate to the people that Saul was His choice. Being obedient to the guidance of the Holy Spirit, can cause any personality shortcoming to be minimized through psychospiritual transformation and inner healing.

Avoidant attachment individuals are able to operate in the gifts of the Spirit when they are under the covering of someone who is spiritually mature.

1 Samuel 10:6-7

The Spirit of the Lord will come upon you in power, and you will prophesy with them; and you will be changed into a different person. ⁷Once these signs are fulfilled, do whatever your hand finds to do, for God is with you.

1 Samuel 10:10-11

When they arrived at Gibeah, a procession of prophets met him; the Spirit of God came upon him in power, and he joined in their prophesying. ¹¹When all those who had formerly known him saw him prophesying with the prophets, they asked each other, "What is this that has happened to the son of Kish? Is Saul also among the prophets?"

1 Samuel 10:10-12

When they arrived at Gibeah, a procession of prophets met him; the Spirit of God came upon him in power, and he joined in their prophesying. ¹¹When all those who had formerly known him saw him prophesying with the prophets, they asked each other, "What is this that has happened to the son of

Kish? Is Saul also among the prophets?" [12]A man who lived there answered, "And who is their father?" So it became a saying: "Is Saul also among the prophets?"

As Saul turned and started to leave, God changed his heart. The prognosis for a psychotherapeutic spiritual formation in a person with avoidant attachment style is guarded, but not bleak.

1 Samuel 10:9
As Saul turned to leave Samuel, God changed Saul's heart, and all these signs were fulfilled that day.

Saul hid. Hiding can be both physical, such as being socially withdrawn and isolative, as well as emotional, which may manifest as being painfully shy. In spite of his impressive physical stature, Saul lacked self-esteem (he was once small in his own eyes) and thought little of himself. Avoidant attachment personalities tend to vacillate in their relational commitment based on the situation.

1 Samuel 10:22
So they inquired further of the Lord, "Has the man come here yet?" And the Lord said, "Yes, he has hidden himself among the baggage."

1 Samuel 15:17
Samuel said, "Although you were once small in your own eyes, did you not become the head of the tribes of Israel? The Lord anointed you king over Israel.

Even though Samuel was there to give instruction and guidance to Saul, because of Saul's avoidant attachment there was not a strong relationship between them, therefore Saul did not

1 Samuel 10:1-12
Then Samuel took a flask of oil and poured it on Saul's head and kissed him, saying, "Has not the Lord anointed you leader over his inheritance? [2]When you leave me today,

commit to following Samuel's instructions. This decision kept Saul's kingdom from being established.

Therapeutic intervention must not only change the cognition or belief system of an avoidant attachment disordered individual, it must also facilitate emotional transformation. The true manifestation of psychospiritual formation is the establishment of reciprocal healthy relationships, both vertical, with God and horizontal, with people.

you will meet two men near Rachel's tomb, at Zelzah on the border of Benjamin. They will say to you, 'The donkeys you set out to look for have been found. And now your father has stopped thinking about them and is worried about you. He is asking, "What shall I do about my son?" '

3"Then you will go on from there until you reach the great tree of Tabor. Three men going up to God at Bethel will meet you there. One will be carrying three young goats, another three loaves of bread, and another a skin of wine. 4They will greet you and offer you two loaves of bread, which you will accept from them. 5"After that you will go to Gibeah of God, where there is a Philistine outpost. As you approach the town, you will meet a procession of prophets coming down from the high place with lyres, tambourines, flutes and harps being played before them, and they will be prophesying. 6The Spirit of the Lord will come upon you in power, and you will prophesy with them; and you will be changed into a different person. 7Once these signs are fulfilled, do whatever your hand finds to do, for God is with you. 8"Go down ahead of me to Gilgal. I will surely come down to you to sacrifice burnt offerings and fellowship offerings, but you must wait seven days until I come to you and tell you what you are to do." [9]As Saul turned to leave Samuel, God changed Saul's heart, and all these signs were fulfilled that day. [10]When they arrived at Gibeah, a procession of prophets met him; the Spirit of God came upon him in power, and he joined in their prophesying. [11]When all those who had formerly known him saw him prophesying with the prophets, they asked each other, "What is this that has happened to the son of Kish? Is Saul also among the prophets?" [12]A man who lived there answered, "And who is their father?" So it became a saying: "Is Saul also among the prophets?"

1 Samuel 13:7-14

Some Hebrews even crossed the Jordan to the land of Gad and Gilead. Saul remained at Gilgal, and all the troops with him were quaking with fear. [8]He waited seven days, the time set by Samuel; but Samuel did not come to Gilgal, and Saul's men began to scatter. [9]So he said, "Bring me the burnt offering and the fellowship offerings." And Saul offered up the burnt offering. [10]Just as he finished making the offering, Samuel arrived, and Saul went out to greet him. [11]"What have you done?" asked Samuel. Saul replied, "When I saw that the men were scattering, and that you did not come at the set time, and that the Philistines were assembling at Micmash, [12]I thought, 'Now the Philistines will come down against me at Gilgal, and I have not sought the Lord's favor.' So I felt compelled to offer the burnt offering." [13]"You acted foolishly," Samuel said. "You have not kept the command the Lord your God gave you; if you had, he would have established your kingdom over Israel for all time. [14]But now your kingdom will not endure; the Lord has sought out a man after his own heart and appointed him leader of his people, because you have not kept the Lord's command."

Saul did not believe Samuel's assessment of him. Avoidant attachment style individuals tend to rationalize, intellectualize, and minimize events that challenge their belief systems. This is a serious problem in counseling, because it hinders the establishment of a therapeutic relationship.

1 Samuel 10:1

Then Samuel took a flask of oil and poured it on Saul's head and kissed him, saying, "Has not the Lord anointed you leader over his inheritance?

1 Samuel 10:16

Saul replied, "He assured us that the donkeys had been

found." But he did not tell his uncle what Samuel had said about the kingship.

Saul probably agreed with their assessment of him and thought, "Who am I to save them?" Because of his poor self-esteem and inhibitions, the peoples' opinion coincided with his self-perceptions.

1 Samuel 10:27
But some troublemakers said, "How can this fellow save us?" They despised him and brought him no gifts. But Saul kept silent.

Saul linked himself with Samuel to give himself credibility. This is another illustration of the insecurity that lies beneath avoidant attachment.

1 Samuel 11:7
He took a pair of oxen, cut them into pieces, and sent the pieces by messengers throughout Israel, proclaiming, "This is what will be done to the oxen of anyone who does not follow Saul and Samuel." Then the terror of the Lord fell on the people, and they turned out as one man.

Saul was to destroy all of the Amalekites and all they had. However, he spared the king and the best of the sheep, oxen and all that was "good." This exemplifies the egocentric and narcissistic traits which places those with avoidant attachment at a higher risk of being disobedient to authority.

1 Samuel 15:3
Now go, attack the Amalekites and totally destroy everything that belongs to them. Do not spare them; put to death men and women, children and infants, cattle and sheep, camels and donkeys.'"

1 Samuel 15:8-9
He took Agag king of the Amalekites alive, and all his people he totally destroyed with

the sword. [9]But Saul and the army spared Agag and the best of the sheep and cattle, the fat calves and lambs—everything that was good. These they were unwilling to destroy completely, but everything that was despised and weak they totally destroyed.

Saul always had an excuse for his disobedience. He felt that partial obedience was sufficient. Those with avoidant attachment style tend to rationalize and justify their irresponsible behavior. Saul's sense of entitlement is typical of the avoidant attachment individual. This sense of pride compelled God to remove His anointing from Saul.

1 Samuel 13:11-12

"What have you done?" asked Samuel. Saul replied, "When I saw that the men were scattering, and that you did not come at the set time, and that the Philistines were assembling at Micmash, [12]I thought, 'Now the Philistines will come down against me at Gilgal, and I have not sought the Lord's favor.' So I felt compelled to offer the burnt offering."

1 Samuel 15:20

"But I did obey the Lord," Saul said. "I went on the mission the Lord assigned me. I completely destroyed the Amalekites and brought back Agag their king.

Because of Samuel, Saul finally admitted his sin and asked for forgiveness but he seemed more concerned with how others would perceive him than with how God

1 Samuel 15:24

Then Saul said to Samuel, "I have sinned. I violated the Lord's command and your instructions. I was afraid of the people and so I gave in to them.

perceived him. This type of attachment puts great emphasis on acceptance by others; therefore, the vertical relationship with God tends to be compromised.

Samuel was afraid Saul might kill him when he went to anoint a new king. Therefore, it seems as though Saul's plea for forgiveness in 1 Samuel 15:25 was not sincere. Samuel's insight was clinically correct in that avoidant attachment individuals are hypersensitive to potential rejection and therefore tend to be reflexively vindictive.	1 Samuel 16:1-2 The Lord said to Samuel, "How long will you mourn for Saul, since I have rejected him as king over Israel? Fill your horn with oil and be on your way; I am sending you to Jesse of Bethlehem. I have chosen one of his sons to be king." ²But Samuel said, "How can I go? Saul will hear about it and kill me." The Lord said, "Take a heifer with you and say, 'I have come to sacrifice to the Lord.'
Saul wanted forgiveness not because he was repentant but because he wanted to avoid the consequences of his behavior. Psychologically this is known as cognitive distortion.	1 Samuel 15:25 Now I beg you, forgive my sin and come back with me, so that I may worship the Lord."
The Spirit of the Lord had left Saul and he was overcome by a tormenting spirit that filled him with depression and fear. Negative traits can be aggravated and magnified to the point that the person who is a perceived threat needs to	1 Samuel 16:14-16 Now the Spirit of the Lord had departed from Saul, and an evil spirit from the Lord tormented him. ¹⁵Saul's attendants said to him, "See, an evil spirit from God is tormenting you. ¹⁶Let

be eliminated.

our lord command his servants here to search for someone who can play the harp. He will play when the evil spirit from God comes upon you, and you will feel better."

1 Samuel 18:10-11
The next day an evil spirit from God came forcefully upon Saul. He was prophesying in his house, while David was playing the harp, as he usually did. Saul had a spear in his hand [11]and he hurled it, saying to himself, "I'll pin David to the wall." But David eluded him twice.

Saul and the people around him knew the problem was that God had left Saul. When an individual is perceived as a source of threat, as David was to Saul, (competition) even though they might have been a source of support or nurturance, the sense of panic to ones' well-being intensifies, as well as the belief that the person needs to be eliminated regardless of ones' relationship with that person.

1 Samuel 16:21
David came to Saul and entered his service. Saul liked him very much, and David became one of his armor-bearers.

Saul liked David because he got something out of the relationship. This is similar to his codependent relationship with his servant.

1 Samuel 16:22-23
Then Saul sent word to Jesse, saying, "Allow David to remain in my service, for I am pleased with him." [23]Whenever

Saul did not believe David could win against Goliath, but he let him go anyway. If David triumphed, it would be to Saul's benefit. This type of personality tends to surround themselves with people who can bolster their shortcomings. They lean upon people to enhance their sense of security and adequacy.

It was almost as though Saul was playing a game by dressing David in grownup armor. People with avoidant relationship style use people for their own self-gain to bolster their own self-confidence and minimize their potential failures.

the spirit from God came upon Saul, David would take his harp and play. Then relief would come to Saul; he would feel better, and the evil spirit would leave him.

1 Samuel 17:33
Saul replied, "You are not able to go out against this Philistine and fight him; you are only a boy, and he has been a fighting man from his youth."

1 Samuel 17:37
"The Lord who delivered me from the paw of the lion and the paw of the bear will deliver me from the hand of this Philistine." Saul said to David, "Go, and the Lord be with you."

1 Samuel 17:38-39
Then Saul dressed David in his own tunic. He put a coat of armor on him and a bronze helmet on his head. [39]David fastened on his sword over the tunic and tried walking around, because he was not used to them. "I cannot go in these," he said to Saul, "because I am not used to them." So he took them off.

Saul may have liked David very much but only because David's music could give him relief. He did not really give David a second thought until after David killed Goliath. For a person with avoidant attachment style, relationships tend to be unidirectional rather than give and take; therefore, each relationship is dysfunctional and short-lived.

1 Samuel 17:55-58

As Saul watched David going out to meet the Philistine, he said to Abner, commander of the army, "Abner, whose son is that young man?" Abner replied, "As surely as you live, O king, I don't know." 56The king said, "Find out whose son this young man is." 57As soon as David returned from killing the Philistine, Abner took him and brought him before Saul, with David still holding the Philistine's head. 58"Whose son are you, young man?" Saul asked him. David said, "I am the son of your servant Jesse of Bethlehem."

Jonathan had relationship with David; Saul did not—although he kept David with him. By contrast Jonathan and David shared mutual respect, acceptance, and willingness to invest in their relationship. This is called a covenant relationship.

1 Samuel 18:2-4

From that day Saul kept David with him and did not let him return to his father's house. 3And Jonathan made a covenant with David because he loved him as himself. 4Jonathan took off the robe he was wearing and gave it to David, along with his tunic, and even his sword, his bow and his belt.

It felt good to Saul to honor David, so long as David did not surpass Saul in the eyes of the people. As previously stated, this type of attachment individual is hypersensitive

1 Samuel 18:5-9

Whatever Saul sent him to do, David did it so successfully that Saul gave him a high rank in the army. This pleased all the people, and Saul's officers to a sense of rejection and has a sense of entitlement. As long as the threat is minimal the relationship can be maintained. Saul was highly sensitive to social pressure. When David received higher praise than Saul, Saul became afraid of him, because David threatened Saul's source of emotional support and sustenance. This type of person vacillates in their level of commitment and oath.

Saul placed David in a situation as commander of a thousand men and he indebted David to himself by giving David his daughter conditionally. The ultimate goal of Saul was the death of David. <u>Indebtedness allows the person with the attachment disorder to retain some emotional control over the other person.</u>

as well. ⁶When the men were returning home after David had killed the Philistine, the women came out from all the towns of Israel to meet King Saul with singing and dancing, with joyful songs and with tambourines and lutes. ⁷As they danced, they sang: "Saul has slain his thousands, and David his tens of thousands." ⁸Saul was very angry; this refrain galled him. They have credited David with tens of thousands, he thought, but me with only thousands. What more can he get but the kingdom? ⁹And from that time on Saul kept a jealous eye on David.

1 Samuel 18:12-17
Saul was afraid of David, because the Lord was with David but had left Saul. ¹³So he sent David away from him and gave him command over a thousand men, and David led the troops in their campaigns. ¹⁴In everything he did he had great success, because the Lord was with him. ¹⁵When Saul saw how successful he was, he was afraid of him. ¹⁶But all Israel and Judah loved David, because he led them in their campaigns. ¹⁷Saul said to David, "Here is my older daughter Merab. I will give her

	to you in marriage; only serve me bravely and fight the battles of the Lord." For Saul said to himself, "I will not raise a hand against him. Let the Philistines do that!"
Saul's avoidant attachment was reinforced when he realized his daughter loved David. He would have perceived Michal's love for David as abandonment.	**1 Samuel 18:28-29** When Saul realized that the Lord was with David and that his daughter Michal loved David, ²⁹Saul became still more afraid of him, and he remained his enemy the rest of his days. **1 Samuel 19:1** Saul told his son Jonathan and all the attendants to kill David. But Jonathan was very fond of David.
Saul took an oath not to kill David. Even Saul realized that he should not try to harm David, although he probably did not perceive that his actions were wrong. Individuals with this type of attachment style lack self-control. Because they lack inner healing or spiritual regeneration, any attempt to exercise self-control is short-lived.	**1 Samuel 19:6-7** Saul listened to Jonathan and took this oath: "As surely as the Lord lives, David will not be put to death." ⁷So Jonathan called David and told him the whole conversation. He brought him to Saul, and David was with Saul as before. **1 Samuel 26:21** Then Saul said, "I have sinned. Come back, David my son. Because you considered my life precious today, I will not try to harm you again. Surely I

have acted like a fool and have erred greatly."

Again, it is after David's success that Saul tries to kill him personally and then sends men to kill him. When Michal, Saul's daughter, warned David, Saul's feelings of abandonment and rejection were reinforced.

1 Samuel 19:8-11

Once more war broke out, and David went out and fought the Philistines. He struck them with such force that they fled before him. [9]But an evil spirit from the Lord came upon Saul as he was sitting in his house with his spear in his hand. While David was playing the harp, [10]Saul tried to pin him to the wall with his spear, but David eluded him as Saul drove the spear into the wall. That night David made good his escape. [11]Saul sent men to David's house to watch it and to kill him in the morning. But Michal, David's wife, warned him, "If you don't run for your life tonight, tomorrow you'll be killed."

When his men did not kill David, Saul asked David to be brought to him, even in his bed, to kill him. Saul's feelings intensified to the point that he was no longer concerned about the perception of others. His actions escalated from putting David in harms way (David did the same thing with Uriah, 2 Sam. 11:15) to commanding others to kill him, to being

1 Samuel 19:15

Then Saul sent the men back to see David and told them, "Bring him up to me in his bed so that I may kill him."

ready to personally kill David. As Saul's feelings intensified, social constraints were not enough to keep his behavior in check.

Three separate times Saul's men went at his request to kill David, but they ended up prophesying when they were under the covering of Samuel and a group of prophets.

1 Samuel 19:18-21

When David had fled and made his escape, he went to Samuel at Ramah and told him all that Saul had done to him. Then he and Samuel went to Naioth and stayed there. [19]Word came to Saul: "David is in Naioth at Ramah"; [20]so he sent men to capture him. But when they saw a group of prophets prophesying, with Samuel standing there as their leader, the Spirit of God came upon Saul's men and they also prophesied. [21]Saul was told about it, and he sent more men, and they prophesied too. Saul sent men a third time, and they also prophesied.

Saul set out presumably to kill David but he too began prophesying under the covering of the prophets at Naioth.

1 Samuel 19:23-24

So Saul went to Naioth at Ramah. But the Spirit of God came even upon him, and he walked along prophesying until he came to Naioth. [24]He stripped off his robes and also prophesied in Samuel's presence. He lay that way all that day and night. This is why people say, "Is Saul also among the prophets?"

Not only was Saul still determined to kill David; his anger had expanded to include those who defended David—even his own son, Jonathan—he was willing to kill them as well. At this point Saul is beyond reasoning with.

1 Samuel 20:30-33

Saul's anger flared up at Jonathan and he said to him, "You son of a perverse and rebellious woman! Don't I know that you have sided with the son of Jesse to your own shame and to the shame of the mother who bore you? ³¹As long as the son of Jesse lives on this earth, neither you nor your kingdom will be established. Now send and bring him to me, for he must die!"

³²"Why should he be put to death? What has he done?" Jonathan asked his father. ³³But Saul hurled his spear at him to kill him. Then Jonathan knew that his father intended to kill David.

1 Samuel 22:14-19

Ahimelech answered the king, "Who of all your servants is as loyal as David, the king's son-in-law, captain of your bodyguard and highly respected in your household? ¹⁵Was that day the first time I inquired of God for him? Of course not! Let not the king accuse your servant or any of his father's family, for your servant knows nothing at all about this whole affair." ¹⁶But the king said, "You will surely die, Ahimelech, you and your father's whole family."

	¹⁷Then the king ordered the guards at his side: "Turn and kill the priests of the Lord, because they too have sided with David. They knew he was fleeing, yet they did not tell me." But the king's officials were not willing to raise a hand to strike the priests of the Lord. ¹⁸The king then ordered Doeg, "You turn and strike down the priests." So Doeg the Edomite turned and struck them down. That day he killed eighty-five men who wore the linen ephod. ¹⁹He also put to the sword Nob, the town of the priests, with its men and women, its children and infants, and its cattle, donkeys and sheep.
Saul calls all the people to war, just to kill David.	1 Samuel 23:8 And Saul called all the people together to war, to go down to Keilah, to besiege David and his men.
	1 Samuel 23:13 So David and his men, about six hundred in number, left Keilah and kept moving from place to place. When Saul was told that David had escaped from Keilah, he did not go there.
Saul was obsessed with killing David. Avoidant attachment	1 Samuel 23:14 David stayed in the desert

individuals obsess over one particular area or person in their life assuming that if this one issue is resolved their life will be problem-free.

strongholds and in the hills of the Desert of Ziph. Day after day Saul searched for him, but God did not give David into his hands.

1 Samuel 23:23

"Find out about all the hiding places he uses and come back to me with definite information. Then I will go with you; if he is in the area, I will track him down among all the clans of Judah."

Saul is truly grieved and gives up the chase, but only temporarily. Note that David does not trust him enough to go with him, but stays in the stronghold. When dealing with people with attachment disorders, be aware of their propensity to act inappropriately.

1 Samuel 24:16-22

When David finished saying this, Saul asked, "Is that your voice, David my son?" And he wept aloud. [17]"You are more righteous than I," he said. "You have treated me well, but I have treated you badly. [18]You have just now told me of the good you did to me; the Lord delivered me into your hands, but you did not kill me. [19]When a man finds his enemy, does he let him get away unharmed? May the Lord reward you well for the way you treated me today. [20]I know that you will surely be king and that the kingdom of Israel will be established in your hands. [21]Now swear to me by the Lord that you will not cut off my descendants or wipe out my name from my father's family."

Saul gave up searching
for David only because
David was out of his reach.
Hypersensitivity and perceived
threats to one's emotional
well-being provoke this type
of attachment style individual
to be highly vindictive; he
has profound difficulty with
forgiveness. Forgiveness of
others cannot occur unless
there is self-love. (Love your
neighbor as yourself, Matt.
22:39.) Devaluation of self and
a chronic sense of emptiness
make self-love almost
impossible to achieve.

Saul failed to consult Samuel
and obey God. In desperation,
he tried to communicate with
Samuel even though Samuel
was dead. Saul's relationship
with Samuel was not based
on honor, respect or love, as

²²So David gave his oath to
Saul. Then Saul returned home,
but David and his men went up
to the stronghold.

1 Samuel 26:2
So Saul went down to the
Desert of Ziph, with his three
thousand chosen men of Israel,
to search there for David.

1 Samuel 27:1-2
But David thought to himself,
"One of these days I will
be destroyed by the hand of
Saul. The best thing I can do
is to escape to the land of the
Philistines. Then Saul will give
up searching for me anywhere
in Israel, and I will slip out of
his hand." ²So David and the
six hundred men with him left
and went over to Achish son of
Maoch king of Gath.

1 Samuel 27:4
When Saul was told that David
had fled to Gath, he no longer
searched for him.

1 Samuel 28:5-20
When Saul saw the Philistine
army, he was afraid; terror
filled his heart. ⁶He inquired
of the Lord, but the Lord did
not answer him by dreams or
Urim or prophets. ⁷Saul then

the prophet of God, but on Saul's sense of entitlement as a king. Saul would do anything to preserve his sense of entitlement and maintain the admiration of his people. Out of desperation he consulted a medium, though he knew this was against the law.

said to his attendants, "Find me a woman who is a medium, so I may go and inquire of her." "There is one in Endor," they said. [8]So Saul disguised himself, putting on other clothes, and at night he and two men went to the woman. "Consult a spirit for me," he said, "and bring up for me the one I name." [9]But the woman said to him, "Surely you know what Saul has done. He has cut off the mediums and spiritists from the land. Why have you set a trap for my life to bring about my death?" [10]Saul swore to her by the Lord, "As surely as the Lord lives, you will not be punished for this." [11]Then the woman asked, "Whom shall I bring up for you?" "Bring up Samuel," he said. [12]When the woman saw Samuel, she cried out at the top of her voice and said to Saul, "Why have you deceived me? You are Saul!" [13]The king said to her, "Don't be afraid. What do you see?" The woman said, "I see a spirit coming up out of the ground." [14]"What does he look like?" he asked. "An old man wearing a robe is coming up," she said. Then Saul knew it was Samuel, and he bowed down and prostrated himself with his face to the ground. [15]Samuel said to Saul, "Why have you disturbed me by bringing me up?" "I am in great distress," Saul said. "The Philistines are fighting against me, and God has turned away from me. He no longer answers me, either by prophets or by dreams. So I have called on you to tell me what to do." [16]Samuel said, "Why do you consult me, now that the Lord has turned away from you and become your enemy? [17]The Lord has done what he predicted through me. The Lord has torn the kingdom out of your hands and given it to one of your neighbors—to David. [18]Because you did not obey the Lord or carry out his fierce wrath against the Amalekites, the Lord has done this to you today. [19]The Lord will hand over both Israel and you to the Philistines, and tomorrow you and your sons will be with me. The Lord will also hand over the army of Israel to the Philistines." [20]Immediately Saul fell full length on the ground, filled with fear because of Samuel's words. His strength was gone, for he had eaten nothing all that day and night.

Saul killed himself. God was his source of secure base attachment, and when the

1 Samuel 31:4-5

Saul said to his armor-bearer, "Draw your sword and run me

Lord took away his anointing, Saul's secure base attachment was gone. When avoidant attachment individuals fully realize the source of secure base attachment is not attainable, their feelings of anguish and helplessness may lead to suicidal behavior. For this type of individual, perseverance is based on external resources rather than strength of character, such we see in the life of Stephen (Acts 7:59-60), who never gave up. Stephen's actions reflected his true psychological transformation.

through, or these uncircumcised fellows will come and run me through and abuse me." But his armor-bearer was terrified and would not do it; so Saul took his own sword and fell on it. [5]When the armor-bearer saw that Saul was dead, he too fell on his sword and died with him.

2 Samuel 1:6-10

"I happened to be on Mount Gilboa," the young man said, "and there was Saul, leaning on his spear, with the chariots and riders almost upon him. [7]When he turned around and saw me, he called out to me, and I said, 'What can I do?'[8]He asked me, 'Who are you?' 'An Amalekite,' I answered. [9]Then he said to me, 'Stand over me and kill me! I am in the throes of death, but I'm still alive.' [10]So I stood over him and killed him, because I knew that after he had fallen he could not survive. And I took the crown that was on his head and the band on his arm and have brought them here to my lord."

Chapter 5

Spiritual Consequences:
Disorganized Attachment

People with disorganized attachment tend to have a combination of anxious ambivalent attachment style and avoidant attachment issues, usually coupled with a traumatic experience.[13] The severity and duration of traumatic experiences tend to influence the severity of disorganized attachment. These individuals tend to be sociopathic. The main feature of a sociopath is lack of conscience. They have no sense of remorse for immoral acts or wrongfulness.

Biblical Examples of Disorganized Attachment

Eli's sons, Hophni and Phinehas, did not receive any discipline, and therefore indulged themselves and used others. There is no data indicating that they were traumatized during their childhood, but their behavior exhibits sociopathic tendencies—meaning they lacked a conscience. They cannot be labeled sociopathic, but they provide biblical	1 Samuel 2:12-17 Eli's sons were wicked men; they had no regard for the Lord. [13]Now it was the practice of the priests with the people that whenever anyone offered a sacrifice and while the meat was being boiled, the servant of the priest would come with a three-pronged fork in his hand. [14]He would plunge it into the pan or kettle or caldron or pot, and the priest would take for himself

---

13 M. Main, N. Kaplin, and J. Cassidy, J, "Security in infancy, childhood, and adulthood: A move to the level of representation," *Monographs for the Society for Research in Child Development* 50 (1985).

examples of that type of behavior.

Eli's sons continued to sin and when Eli finally decided to discipline them it was too little, too late. The timing of discipline is extremely important. The old behaviors need to be extinguished and new behaviors need to be learned. These issues can be avoided if the child is disciplined early in life.

whatever the fork brought up. This is how they treated all the Israelites who came to Shiloh. ¹⁵But even before the fat was burned, the servant of the priest would come and say to the man who was sacrificing, "Give the priest some meat to roast; he won't accept boiled meat from you, but only raw." ¹⁶If the man said to him, "Let the fat be burned up first, and then take whatever you want," the servant would then answer, "No, hand it over now; if you don't, I'll take it by force." ¹⁷This sin of the young men was very great in the Lord's sight, for they were treating the Lord's offering with contempt.

1 Samuel 2:22-25

Now Eli, who was very old, heard about everything his sons were doing to all Israel and how they slept with the women who served at the entrance to the Tent of Meeting. ²³So he said to them, "Why do you do such things? I hear from all the people about these wicked deeds of yours. ²⁴No, my sons; it is not a good report that I hear spreading among the Lord's people. ²⁵If a man sins against another man, God may mediate for him; but if a man sins against the Lord, who will intercede for him?" His sons, however, did not listen to their father's rebuke, for it was the Lord's will to put them to death.

1 Samuel 2:29

Why do you scorn my sacrifice and offering that I prescribed for my dwelling? Why do you honor your sons more than me by fattening yourselves on the choice parts of every offering made by my people Israel?"

1 Samuel 2:34

"And what happens to your two sons, Hophni and Phinehas, will be a sign to you—they will both die on the same day.

1 Samuel 3:13-14

"For I told him that I would judge his family forever because of the sin he knew about; his sons made themselves contemptible, and he failed to restrain them. [14]Therefore, I swore to the house of Eli, 'The guilt of Eli's house will never be atoned for by sacrifice or offering.'"

1 Samuel 4:14-17

Eli heard the outcry and asked, "What is the meaning of this uproar?" The man hurried over to Eli, [15]who was ninety-eight years old and whose eyes were set so that he could not see. [16]He told Eli, "I have just come from the battle line; I

	fled from it this very day." Eli asked, "What happened, my son?" [17]The man who brought the news replied, "Israel fled before the Philistines, and the army has suffered heavy losses. Also your two sons, Hophni and Phinehas, are dead, and the ark of God has been captured."

Individuals with disorganized attachment have such an under-developed conscience that they do not experience remorse or guilt for their wrongdoing. They rationalize their behavior and more importantly, they tend to project blame onto others for such predicaments. Since they function more on the intellectual level, the rationale can be very compelling. Prognosis for psychotherapeutic intervention is extremely guarded due to the lack of remorse or lack of willingness to acknowledge culpability for one's wrong doing. If there is any admission of guilt it tends to be at the cognitive level, and thereby short lived, without behavior changes. King David recognized his moral failure of committing murder, being cognitively aware when he was confronted by the prophet Nathan (2 Sam. 12). After this confrontation there was emotional remorse and behaviorally overt changes which are exemplified in the way he parented Solomon. This is an example of true repentance. Unfortunately, with disorganized attachment disordered individuals, this type of genuine admission of guilt is profoundly difficult.

The majority of sociopaths are very intelligent. They have a sense of entitlement and the need to be in control. The need for control ultimately stems from them attempting to prevent any real or perceived victimization. When they do feel victimized, or even feel they are being taken advantage of, these individuals become angry and engage in inappropriate behavior as a means of getting even. This could include stealing, sexual imposition, being under productive, and murder. Compassion, self-sacrifice, and minimal pay reinforce the feelings of victimization; therefore, these individuals would not be likely to enter into a profession of helping.

Chapter 6

Psychospiritual Healing

Generational sin affects physical, emotional, and spiritual development. Cortisol is a stress hormone. Low cortisol is a vulnerability marker for posttraumatic stress disorder (PTSD). By looking at Nazi Holocaust survivors, their offspring, and the presence of PTSD, researchers in New York City have found biological evidence of the intergenerational transmission of stress vulnerability.[14] Genes in each cell's nucleus store a vast amount of information, including instructions concerning how to function in certain situations and when to stop functioning, i.e., growth of breasts or facial hair during puberty. The wealth of information that genes contain is encoded on DNA within the cells. This may be how the issues of Exodus 20 "generational sin" or "generational blessing" are transferred from one generation to another.

> **Exodus 20:5-6**
>
> You shall not bow down to them or worship them; for I, the Lord your God, am a jealous God, punishing the children for the sin of the fathers to the third and fourth generation of those who hate me, ⁶but showing love to a thousand generations of those who love me and keep my commandments.

---

14 R. Yehuda, J. Schmeidler, M. Wainberg, K. Binder-Brynes, and T. Duvdevani, "Vulnerability to posttraumatic stress disorder in adult offspring of Holocaust survivors," *American Journal of Psychiatry* 155 (1998): 1163-71.

Exodus 34:7 (The Amplified Bible)

Keeping mercy and loving-kindness for thousands, forgiving iniquity and transgression and sin, but Who will by no means clear the guilty, visiting the iniquity of the fathers upon the children and the children's children, to the third and fourth generation.

Only 5 to 10 percent of the human genes are known to be active every minute, if they stop working death occurs instantly. What the rest are actually doing remains unknown. The fact that psychological states can change the way genes function may actually be possible because so many genes are dormant. The "joy of the Lord" can change your genes. A change of environment can trigger changes in your genes. Laughter has a beneficial effect on blood-glucose levels, twenty-three genes were activated from laughing.[15, 16]

Everyone carries the spiritual DNA of generational behavioral patterns. In clinical psychology, this is referred to as "family pathology." Through the process of "contemplative prayer," "scriptural meditation," and "practicing His presence" the Holy Spirit will give insight to the parent as to how their own generational pathology is a hindrance to a loving relationship with the Father as well as the adopted child. This process will also allow insight into the generational sins of the adopted child enabling the parent to meet the child's needs. Consciously entering into the presence of God transforms and renews man. In doing so, John 3:30 is accomplished, "He (Christ) must increase, but I must decrease."

With the eradication of the generational pathology, the following can be accomplished:

---

15 K. Hayashi, T. Hayashi, S. Iwanaga, K. Kawai, H. Ishii, S. Shoji, and K. Murakami, "Laughter lowered the increase in postprandial blood glucose," *Diabetes Care* 26 (2003): 1651-52.

16 L. S. Berk, S. A. Tan, W. F. Fry, B. J. Napier, J. W. Lee, R. W. Hubbard, J. E. Lewis, and W. C. Eby, "Neuroendocrine and stress hormone changes during mirthful laughter," *American Journal of Medical Science* 298 (December 1989): 390-96.

Matthew 22:37 (AMP)

And He replied to him, You shall love the Lord your God with all your heart and with all your soul and with all your mind (intellect).

The brain's final wiring is only going to be connected up, consolidated, and smoothly established in accordance with how it is used in the course of subsequent development or experiences. Benefits from the experiences are possible since the brain is malleable or changeable, but more importantly, the experience is encoded in DNA and it becomes possible to pass on the qualities that have been acquired to the next generations. Theological, this may be called "generational iniquitous behavioral patterns" or "generational blessings."

Ephesians 4:22 (AMP)

Strip yourselves of your former nature [put off and discard your old unrenewed self] which characterized your previous manner of life and becomes corrupt through lusts and desires that spring from delusion;

This is not limited to spiritual development but also to the very fabric of one's physical being, genetics. Research reflects that a "supportive environment" [loving, nurturing relationship] reverses the impact of a genetic risk factor.[17]

I Kings 19:7

The angel of the LORD came back a second time and touched him and said, "Get up and eat, for the journey is too much for you.

---

17 University of California - Los Angeles (2006, October 13). Early Family Experience Can Reverse The Effects Of Genes, Psychologists Report. *Science Daily*. Retrieved January 5, 2009, from http://www.sciencedaily.com /releases/2006/10/061012190132.htm.

The nurturing interaction between Elijah and the angel healed his clinical syndrome of Acute Distress Disorder which is a psychoneurobiological condition. In light of the encounter with Jezebel and the prophets of Baal, Elijah suffered acute psychophysiological burnout which was due to the stress hormone negatively impacting his physical, psychological, and spiritual functioning.

Mothers have long carried the responsibilities of their unborn child's health, e.g., don't drink [Fetal Alcohol Syndrome], don't smoke [nicotine exposure in utero enhances the risk of ADHD]. Studies demonstrate that fathers exposed to drugs, alcohol, radiation, solvent, etc. can also lead to medical/behavioral pathologies. Low birth weight infants have a higher risk of developing coronary heart disease in later life and up to half of adult diseases may be linked to developmental causes.[18] Studies with rats indicate that frequent maternal licking and grooming of the young increases cognitive and social skills as well as lowering stress.[19] This holds true even if the young rat is from a less-affectionate mother and is placed with an affectionate "adoptive" mother.[20] The implications of this are that the adoptive parents can have an impact on the child's development. The genetic imprint of Exodus 20 is modifiable via "early" nurturing relationships.

What about if the individual is an adult? Research on "retrocausal" effects [time reversed effects] experiments supports retroactive influence on living systems. Nineteen studies involving 233 individual sessions produced odds against chance of ten million to one that time reversal effects could occur.[21]

Chemical modifications to DNA and proteins can change the way genes are packaged and regulated without changing the genes themselves. Epigenetic modifications, the environment influencing substance and behavior, act as a molecular scrapbook, preserving memories of events in parents' lives and handing them down to the next generation and beyond. That memory is established in

18 M. Price, "Programmed for life?" *Monitor on Psychology* 40 (February 2009): 29-31.

19 M. Price, "Programmed for life?" *Monitor on Psychology* 40 (February 2009): 29-31.

20 M. Price, "Programmed for life?" *Monitor on Psychology* 40 (February 2009): 29-31.

21 W. Braud, "Wellness implications of retroactive intentional influence: Exploring an outrageous hypothesis," *Alternative Therapies* 6 (January 2000): 37-48.

the form of a chemical marker called methylation.[22] Epigenetic research has established that DNA blueprints passed down through genes are not set at birth. Environmental influences such as nutrition, stress, and emotions can modify those genes without changing the basic blueprints. These modifications can be passed on to future generations via DNA.[23, 24] Research on information-processing receptors on nerve cell membranes indicates that the same "neural" receptors are present on most, it not all, of the body's cells. The "mind" is not focused solely in the head or brain but is distributed via signal molecules to the whole body.[25]

Research in the field of child maltreatment has uncovered intergenerational patterns of abuse,[26] or generational sin. Approximately 30 percent of parents who experienced maltreatment in childhood will commit abusive behavior on their own offspring.[27] To explain this pattern psychologists focus on learning and attachment models.[28] When abused children become parents, they model their parenting behavior on what they observed and learned from their own parents.[29] Attachment theory is another theoretical paradigm used to explain generational psychopathology.[30] When people are victimized as children, they often spend years living with negative emotions. New sets of behavior need to be learned. At this juncture of the person's life, such a change requires re-parenting. Generational psychopathology (generational sin) operates in the lives of many Christian families. Before people

---

22 A. Bird, "DNA methylation patterns and epigenetic memory," *Genes & Development* 16 (January 2002): 6-21.

23 M. Surani, "Reprogramming of genome function through epigenetic inheritance," *Nature* 414 (2001): 122.

24 W. Reik and J. Walter, 2001, "Genomic imprinting: Parental influence on the genome," *Nature Reviews Genetics* 2 (2001): 21.

25 C. Pert, *Molecules of Emotion* (New York: Touchstone, 1997).

26 S. Zuravin, C. McMillen, D. DePanfilis and C. Risley-Curtiss, "The intergenerational cycle of child maltreatment," *Journal of Interpersonal Violence* 11 (1996).

27 J. Kaufman, and E. Zigler, "Do abused children become abusive parents?" *American Journal of Orthopsychiatry* 57 (1987).

28 C. George, "A representational perspective of child abuse and prevention: Internal working models of attachment and caregiving," *Child Abuse and Neglect* 20 (1996).

29 R. Muller, J. Hunter and G. Stollak, "The intergenerational transmission of corporal punishment: A comparison of social learning and temperament models," *Child Abuse and Neglect* 19 (1995).

30 S. Zuravin, C. McMillen, D. DePanfilis and C. Risley-Curtiss, "The intergenerational cycle of child maltreatment," *Journal of Interpersonal Violence* 11 (1996).

begin the process of re-parenting, they need to ask the Holy Spirit for inner spiritual healing. This procedure requires divine guidance to help understand the impact of childhood experiences on their psychospiritual development. Secondly, there must be willingness to forgive the parents' shortcomings, whether the wrongdoing was premeditated or not. Forgiveness is essential in this type of progressive journey to spiritual maturity. Forgiveness does not mean forgetting what was done; instead, it means releasing the impact of the wrong actions, including anger, hatred, and pain. As the apostle Paul noted in Colossians 3:5, "put to death ... what is earthly in you... ." The Greek word for forgiveness is *apheine,* which conveys the idea "to let go, put away, omit, send away."[31]

The Complete Word Study Dictionary New Testament tells us that *apheseos* means "to cause to stand away from, to release one's sins from the sinner. Forgiveness, remission. This required Christ's sacrifice as punishment of sin, hence the putting away of sin and the deliverance for the sinner from the power of sin, although not from its presence, which will come later after the resurrection when our very bodies will be redeemed."[32]

Forgiveness is more than a one-time effort. It is a process that requires a continual effort of letting go until the residual impact of the event is totally healed. Additionally, forgiveness does not depend on repentance from the offender. The underlying common denominator of forgiveness is to facilitate "healing of a broken relationship." Forgiveness is a conscious, purposeful action to eliminate emotions that keep us from a covenant relationship with God. It means changing the way of thinking and feeling toward people who caused the hurt. The primary ingredients of forgiveness are:

a) The one who forgives has suffered a deep hurt, thus showing resentment.

b) The offended person has a moral right to resentment, but overcomes it.

---

31 S. Zodhiates, *The Complete Word Study Dictionary New Testament* (Chattanooga, TN: AMG International, Inc., 1993).

32 S. Zodhiates, *The Complete Word Study Dictionary New Testament* (Chattanooga, TN: AMG International, Inc., 1993), 296.

c) A new response to the other accrues, including compassion and love.

d) This loving response occurs, despite the realization that there is no obligation to love the offender. [33]

In the Lord's Prayer, asking God to forgive is linked to the ability to forgive others. In fact, in Matthew 6, Jesus indicates that forgiving those who transgress will bring forgiveness. If forgiveness is withheld God will withhold His forgiveness. Forgiveness implies submission to the sovereign authority of God as judge and ruler over all human offenses.

The first goal of forgiveness is freedom for the victim, providing him with the ability to mature as a believer. The second goal is reconciliation, which may eventually lead to restoration of relationship. John 13:34 states: "A new command I give you: Love one another. As I have loved you, so you must love one another." This verse mandates reconciliation, which literally means to "bring together again." Forgiveness requires only one person, while reconciliation takes two—the victim and the offender. Restoration of the relationship is a bi-directional interaction as well as a process. The process can bring about progressive healing.

Unfortunately, achieving restoration takes time and persistent effort. If the offense was mild, the time it takes to forgive and eventually reconcile may be relatively short. In contrast, if the offense was intense and significant, forgiving the culpable person will take great effort, and reconciliation may not occur for years, if at all. In any case, forgiveness is the first step. An illustration of this principle is seen in the life of Joseph. After Joseph's brothers abandoned him, twenty years passed before they met again (Gen. 42). Joseph did not acknowledge them as his brothers right away, but by the time they returned he was ready to begin the process of forgiveness and reconciliation.

The process of forgiveness often sets the victim free from the sequela of unforgiveness: anger, hurt, depression, and bitterness.

---

33 M. Subkoviak, R. Enright, C. R. Wu, E. Gassin, S. Freedman, L. Olson, & I. Sarinopoulos, I. "Measuring interpersonal forgiveness" (paper presented at the annual meeting of the American Educational Research Association, San Francisco, California, April, 1992).

Colossians 3:13

Bear with each other and forgive whatever grievances you may have against one another. Forgive as the Lord forgave you.

Ephesians 4:32

Be kind and compassionate to one another, forgiving each other, just as in Christ God forgave you.

Psalm 4:4

In your anger do not sin; when you are on your beds, search your hearts and be silent.

Psalm 37:8

Refrain from anger and turn from wrath; do not fret--it leads only to evil.

Proverbs 29:8

Mockers stir up a city, but wise men turn away anger.

Proverbs 29:11

A fool gives full vent to his anger, but a wise man keeps himself under control.

Proverbs 30:33

For as churning the milk produces butter, and as twisting the nose produces blood, so stirring up anger produces strife.

Ecclesiastes 7:9

Do not be quickly provoked in your spirit, for anger resides in the lap of fools.

Ecclesiastes 10:4

If a ruler's anger rises against you, do not leave your post; calmness can lay great errors to rest.

2 Corinthians 12:20

For I am afraid that when I come I may not find you as I want you to be, and you may not find me as you want me to be. I fear that there may be quarreling, jealousy, outbursts of anger, factions, slander, gossip, arrogance and disorder.

Ephesians 4:31

Get rid of all bitterness, rage and anger, brawling and slander, along with every form of malice.

Colossians 3:8

But now you must rid yourselves of all such things as these: anger, rage, malice, slander, and filthy language from your lips.

John Mark had conflicting ideas with the missionary team, to take the gospel elsewhere. Uncle Barnabas wanted to take his nephew when the team went back for a second time. Paul had not yet reconciled with Mark and would not take Mark on his team (Acts 15:36-39). However, forgiveness, reconciliation, and eventually restoration of the relationship came later as noted in 2 Timothy 4:11, "Only Luke is with me. Get Mark and bring him with you, because he is helpful to me in my ministry."

Restoring a relationship requires progressive healing. With grace and mercy, the broken relationship can progress to a covenant relationship between the offended and the offender.

Forgiveness

In order to receive forgiveness, the believer must first forgive. Christians have the power to forgive.	Matthew 6:12-15 Forgive us our debts, as we also have forgiven our debtors. [13]And lead us not into temptation, but deliver us from the evil one.' [14]For if you forgive men when they sin against you, your heavenly Father will also forgive you. [15]But if you do not forgive men their sins, your Father will not forgive your sins. Mark 11:25 And when you stand praying, if you hold anything against anyone, forgive him, so that your Father in heaven may forgive you your sins. Luke 6:37 Do not judge, and you will not be judged. Do not condemn, and you will not be condemned. Forgive, and you will be forgiven. James 1:19-20 My dear brothers, take note of this: Everyone should be quick to listen, slow to speak and slow to become angry, [20]for man's anger does not bring about the righteous life that God desires.
Unforgiveness reinforces the consequences of generational pathology, such as depression,	Luke 11:4 Forgive us our sins, for we also forgive everyone who sins

anxiety, anger, and other mental health issues.

Forgiveness applies to believers and nonbelievers. Believers are to forgive as they have been forgiven.

against us. And lead us not into temptation.

John 20:23

If you forgive anyone his sins, they are forgiven; if you do not forgive them, they are not forgiven."

Matthew 18:21-35

Then Peter came to Jesus and asked, "Lord, how many times shall I forgive my brother when he sins against me? Up to seven times?" [22]Jesus answered, "I tell you, not seven times, but seventy-seven times.

[23]"Therefore, the kingdom of heaven is like a king who wanted to settle accounts with his servants. [24]As he began the settlement, a man who owed him ten thousand talents was brought to him. [25]Since he was not able to pay, the master ordered that he and his wife and his children and all that he had be sold to repay the debt. [26]"The servant fell on his knees before him. 'Be patient with me,' he begged, 'and I will pay back everything.' [27]The servant's master took pity on him, canceled the debt and let him go. [28]"But when that servant went out, he found one of his fellow servants who owed him a hundred denarii. He grabbed him and began

to choke him. 'Pay back what you owe me!' he demanded. [29]"His fellow servant fell to his knees and begged him, 'Be patient with me, and I will pay you back.' [30]"But he refused. Instead, he went off and had the man thrown into prison until he could pay the debt. [31]When the other servants saw what had happened, they were greatly distressed and went and told their master everything that had happened. [32]"Then the master called the servant in. 'You wicked servant,' he said, 'I canceled all that debt of yours because you begged me to. [33]Shouldn't you have had mercy on your fellow servant just as I had on you?' [34]In anger his master turned him over to the jailers to be tortured, until he should pay back all he owed. [35]"This is how my heavenly Father will treat each of you unless you forgive your brother from your heart."

Believers are to forgive the same person again and again, if he says "I repent" forgive him even if it is several times a day. There are times when forgiveness is conditional upon the person's repentance, nevertheless it is far more preferable to fully forgive and eliminate the risk of bitterness being the seed toward generational sin.

Luke 17:3-4

So watch yourselves. "If your brother sins, rebuke him, and if he repents, forgive him. [4]If he sins against you seven times in a day, and seven times comes back to you and says, 'I repent,' forgive him."

Forgiveness does not mean immediately re-establishing a relationship.	2 Corinthians 2:5-11 If anyone has caused grief, he has not so much grieved me as he has grieved all of you, to some extent—not to put it too severely. ⁶The punishment inflicted on him by the majority is sufficient for him. ⁷Now instead, you ought to forgive and comfort him, so that he will not be overwhelmed by excessive sorrow. ⁸I urge you, therefore, to reaffirm your love for him. ⁹The reason I wrote you was to see if you would stand the test and be obedient in everything. ¹⁰If you forgive anyone, I also forgive him. And what I have forgiven—if there was anything to forgive—I have forgiven in the sight of Christ for your sake, ¹¹in order that Satan might not outwit us. For we are not unaware of his schemes.
The person who is sinning should be held accountable.	Matthew 18:15-17 If your brother sins against you, go and show him his fault, just between the two of you. If he listens to you, you have won your brother over. ¹⁶But if he will not listen, take one or two others along, so that 'every matter may be established by the testimony of two or three witnesses.' ¹⁷If he refuses to listen to them, tell it to the church; and if he refuses to listen even to the church, treat him as you would a pagan or a tax collector.

Forgiveness does not mean associating with others.	1 Corinthians 5:11 But now I am writing you that you must not associate with anyone who calls himself a brother but is sexually immoral or greedy, an idolater or a slanderer, a drunkard or a swindler. With such a man do not even eat.
Forgive as the Lord forgives.	Colossians 3:13 Bear with each other and forgive whatever grievances you may have against one another. Forgive as the Lord forgave you.
Inner healing is a process; therefore, it does not need to be fully completed before re-parenting can begin. Elijah re-parented Samuel, even though he was still dealing with his wayward sons.	1 Peter 2:2 Like newborn babies, crave pure spiritual milk, so that by it you may grow up in your salvation,
Inner healing is eradicating the emotional consequences of attachment disorders.	2 Corinthians 5:17 Therefore, if anyone is in Christ, he is a new creation; the old has gone, the new has come!
Psychospiritual rehabilitation occurs when the inner world of a person is in alignment with the reality of Jesus Christ, as Lord and savior.	Colossians 1:13 For he has rescued us from the dominion of darkness and brought us into the kingdom of the Son he loves,
The Lordship of Christ, the God of the Hebrew Scriptures, is essential and necessary as the primary foundation to psychospiritual formation of a	Philippians 2:9-11 Therefore God exalted him to the highest place and gave him the name that is above every name, [10]that at the name of Jesus every

healthy personality.

knee should bow, in heaven and on earth and under the earth, [11]and every tongue confess that Jesus Christ is Lord, to the glory of God the Father.

Prayer as a form of therapeutic intervention must be utilized with the consent of the other person and active participation to receive divine healing.

Matthew 14:13-14

When Jesus heard what had happened, he withdrew by boat privately to a solitary place. Hearing of this, the crowds followed him on foot from the towns. [14]When Jesus landed and saw a large crowd, he had compassion on them and healed their sick.

Formational counseling/ spiritual re-parenting depends on the Holy Spirit and Jesus Christ. Character transformation cannot occur without being regenerated by the Holy Spirit.

John 15:5

"I am the vine; you are the branches. If a man remains in me and I in him, he will bear much fruit; apart from me you can do nothing.

Once the primary hindrance to inner healing such as generational sins, curses, or pathology is eradicated through the power of prayer, in the name of our Lord and Savior, then psychospiritual rehabilitation can proceed via re-parenting.

Romans 8:37

No, in all these things we are more than conquerors through him who loved us.

2 Corinthians 10:4-5

The weapons we fight with are not the weapons of the world. On the contrary, they have divine power to demolish strongholds. [5]We demolish arguments and every pretension that sets itself up against the knowledge of God, and we take captive every thought to make it obedient to Christ.

One of the major benefits of forgiveness is subtle; it relates to research showing that people with strong social networks—of friends, neighbors, and family—tend to be healthier than loners. Someone who nurses grudges and keeps track of every slight is obviously going to shed some relationships over the course of a lifetime. *Forgiveness means overcoming negative feelings and judgment toward the offender.*

Psychological experiences, especially during childhood, have a tremendous impact on spiritual growth to maturity (defining maturity as a strong interpersonal relationship with God). The New Testament admonishes the older woman to re-parent the younger women as reflected in:

Titus 2:3-5

Likewise, teach the older women to be reverent in the way they live, not to be slanderers or addicted to much wine, but to teach what is good. ⁴Then they can train the younger women to love their husbands and children, ⁵to be self–controlled and pure, to be busy at home, to be kind, and to be subject to their husbands, so that no one will malign the word of God.

Re-parenting is the biblical mode of therapeutic intervention—a way to offset the negative impact of inconsistent parenting resulting in attachment disorder. Physical healing for the child's DNA is also warranted. Distant healing [intercessory prayer] can alter the rate of winding and unwinding strands of DNA.[34] The implications of these studies are far reaching. This could be the mechanism for the action of healing within the body since DNA controls many of the function of cells in the body. Parents must pray for spiritual, emotional, and physical healing for the child that needs re-parenting.

---

34 G. Rein and R. McCraty, "Structual changes in water and DNA associated with new physiologically measurable states," *Journal of Scientific Exploration*, 8 (1995): 438-39.

Chapter 7

Relational Empowerment

Empowerment led by the Holy Spirit is essential to healing. People who suffer from attachment disorders have a sense of helplessness which precludes them from believing their prayers will be answered. Furthermore, this sense of hopelessness prevents them from asking our divine Father for assistance. Children who are avoidant, having experienced repeated losses and separations from their primary caregiver, pray less when experiencing stress.[35] Avoidant individuals experience closeness as a sense of discomfort and therefore avoid prayer when under stress.[36] Anxious ambivalent adults do not avoid prayer but engage in "help-seeking" behavior which could include petitionary, materialistic prayer.[37, 38] In contrast, secure base attached individuals pray when they are under stress but they are most likely seeking emotional closeness as opposed to material answers in response to their prayer.[39]

By providing anointed empowerment, re-parenting can bestow hope, self-confidence, and the ability to overcome the biological parents' generational sins of inappropriate parenting. Spiritual empowerment means using God-given authority to eliminate whatever hindrance prevents an individual from acquiring the

35 R. Jubis, "An attachment theoretical approach to understanding children's conceptions of God," (unpublished doctoral dissertation, University of Denver, Denver, Colorado, 1991).

36 K. Bird and A. Boe, "The correspondence between attachment dimensions and prayer in college students," *International Journal for the Psychology of Religion* 11 (2001): 9-24.

37 K. Bird and A. Boe, "The correspondence between attachment dimensions and prayer in college students," *International Journal for the Psychology of Religion* 11 (2001): 9-24.

38 O. Pettern, M. West, A. Mahoney and A. Keller, "Depression and attachment problems," *Journal of Psychiatry and Neuroscience* 18 (1993): 78-81.

39 K. Bird and A. Boe, "The correspondence between attachment dimensions and prayer in college students," *International Journal for the Psychology of Religion* 11 (2001): 9-24.

"fruit of the spirit." Empowerment operating in a person's life brings a feeling of psychospiritual well-being. At this juncture of re-parenting, the person feels a sense of being able to belong to the fellowship, kononia. Empowerment consists of the following:

1. Community involvement, including leadership responsibilities.[40, 41] This would be the implementation of "forsake not the fellowship." One of the fivefold ministries is operational.

Hebrews 10:25

Let us not give up meeting together, as some are in the habit of doing, but let us encourage one another—and all the more as you see the Day approaching.

Romans 12:6-8

We have different gifts, according to the grace given us. If a man's gift is prophesying, let him use it in proportion to his faith. [7]If it is serving, let him serve; if it is teaching, let him teach; [8]if it is encouraging, let him encourage; if it is contributing to the needs of others, let him give generously; if it is leadership, let him govern diligently; if it is showing mercy, let him do it cheerfully.

I Corinthians 12:28

And in the church God has appointed first of all apostles, second prophets, third teachers, then workers of miracles, also those having gifts of healing, those able to help others, those with gifts of administration, and those speaking in different kinds of tongues.

40 Cornell Empowerment Group, "Empowerment through family framework," *Networking Bulletin: Empowerment and family support* 1 (1989).

41 M. Zimmerman and J. Rappaport, "Citizens participation, perceived control and psychological empowerment," *American Journal of Community Psychology* 16 (1988).

2. Acquiring effective problem solving skills, coping strategies, and the ability to utilize available resources.[42, 43, 44] This is the manifestation of the "fruit of the spirit" and includes the ability to wage spiritual warfare.

Galatians 5:22-23

But the fruit of the Spirit is love, joy, peace, patience, kindness, goodness, faithfulness, [23]gentleness and self-control. Against such things there is no law.

2 Corinthians 10:3-6

For though we live in the world, we do not wage war as the world does. [4]The weapons we fight with are not the weapons of the world. On the contrary, they have divine power to demolish strongholds. [5]We demolish arguments and every pretension that sets itself up against the knowledge of God, and we take captive every thought to make it obedient to Christ. [6]And we will be ready to punish every act of disobedience, once your obedience is complete.

I Timothy 1:18-19

Timothy, my son, I give you this instruction in keeping with the prophecies once made about you, so that by following them you may fight the good fight, [19]holding on to faith and a good conscience. Some have rejected these and so have shipwrecked their faith.

Ephesians 6:10-12

Finally, be strong in the Lord and in his mighty power. [11]Put on the full armor of God so that you can take your stand against the devil's schemes.

---

42 *Cognitive coping, families and disability*, ed. A. Turnbull, J. Patterson, S. Behr, D. Murphy, J. Marquis, and M. Blue-Banning (Baltimore: Brookes, 1993).

43 M. Cochran, "Parent empowerment: Developing a conceptual framework," *Science Review* 5 (1992).

44 K. Heller, "Social and community interventions," *Annual Review of Psychology* 41 (1990).

¹²For our struggle is not against flesh and blood, but against the rulers, against the authorities, against the powers of this dark world and against the spiritual forces of evil in the heavenly realms.

3. Collaboration,[45] or the ability to establish a divine alliance within the fivefold ministry gifts.

Paul's relationship with Timothy shows a pattern of spiritual re-parenting that can be used as a model.

Paul's Pattern of Re–parenting

A Parent's Responsibility to the Child	
Parents must first turn their hearts to their child.	Malachi 4:6 He will turn the hearts of the fathers to their children, and the hearts of the children to their fathers; or else I will come and strike the land with a curse."
Be committed to pray for him.	2 Timothy 1:1-3 Paul, an apostle of Christ Jesus by the will of God, according to the promise of life that is in Christ Jesus, ²To Timothy, my dear son: Grace, mercy and peace from God the Father and Christ Jesus our Lord. ³I thank God, whom I serve, as my forefathers did, with a clear conscience, as night and day I constantly remember you in my prayers.

---

45 M. Fine, "Facilitating home-school relationship: A family oriented approach to collaborative consultation," *Journal of Education and Psychological Consultation* 1 (1990).

Encourage him. Paul gave Timothy instructions so that it would encourage him to keep going.	1 Timothy 1:18-19 Timothy, my son, I give you this instruction in keeping with the prophecies once made about you, so that by following them you may fight the good fight, [19]holding on to faith and a good conscience. Some have rejected these and so have shipwrecked their faith.
Always look out for his physical well-being.	1 Timothy 5:23 Stop drinking only water, and use a little wine because of your stomach and your frequent illnesses.
Interact with his circle of friends and family; it appears Paul was familiar with Timothy's mother and grandmother.	2 Timothy 1:5 I have been reminded of your sincere faith, which first lived in your grandmother Lois and in your mother Eunice and, I am persuaded, now lives in you also.
He should interact with the parent's circle of people.	2 Timothy 4:19 Greet Priscilla and Aquila and the household of Onesiphorus. 2 Timothy 4:21 Do your best to get here before winter. Eubulus greets you, and so do Pudens, Linus, Claudia and all the brothers.

Attachment disorder individuals need a great deal of grace and tolerance from those around them.	1 Timothy 6:21b Grace be with you.
Desire to be With the Child, Express These Warm Feelings Express your desire to spend time with him.	1 Timothy 3:14-15 Although I hope to come to you soon, I am writing you these instructions so that, [15]if I am delayed, you will know how people ought to conduct themselves in God's household, which is the church of the living God, the pillar and foundation of the truth. 2 Timothy 1:4 Recalling your tears, I long to see you, so that I may be filled with joy. 2 Timothy 4:9 Do your best to come to me quickly,
Use words of endearment and encouragement.	2 Timothy 2:1 You then, my son, be strong in the grace that is in Christ Jesus.
Responsibility of the Child to the Parent Keep him informed on other aspects of the ministry as well as asking him to do things that are practical (bring my cloak,	2 Timothy 4:10-22 For Demas, because he loved this world, has deserted me and has gone to Thessalonica. Crescens has gone to Galatia, and Titus to Dalmatia. [11]Only

books and papers) and give messages to others.

Luke is with me. Get Mark and bring him with you, because he is helpful to me in my ministry. ¹²I sent Tychicus to Ephesus. ¹³When you come, bring the cloak that I left with Carpus at Troas, and my scrolls, especially the parchments. ¹⁴Alexander the metalworker did me a great deal of harm. The Lord will repay him for what he has done. ¹⁵You too should be on your guard against him, because he strongly opposed our message. ¹⁶At my first defense, no one came to my support, but everyone deserted me. May it not be held against them. ¹⁷But the Lord stood at my side and gave me strength, so that through me the message might be fully proclaimed and all the Gentiles might hear it. And I was delivered from the lion's mouth. ¹⁸The Lord will rescue me from every evil attack and will bring me safely to his heavenly kingdom. To him be glory for ever and ever. Amen. ¹⁹Greet Priscilla and Aquila and the household of Onesiphorus. ²⁰Erastus stayed in Corinth, and I left Trophimus sick in Miletus. ²¹Do your best to get here before winter. Eubulus greets you, and so do Pudens, Linus, Claudia and all the brothers. ²²The Lord be with your spirit. Grace be with you.

Encourage him to hold onto, remember, and carefully guard what he has learned. Expect him to learn to listen to God.	**2 Timothy 1:13-14** What you heard from me, keep as the pattern of sound teaching, with faith and love in Christ Jesus. [14]Guard the good deposit that was entrusted to you—guard it with the help of the Holy Spirit who lives in us. **2 Timothy 2:7** Reflect on what I am saying, for the Lord will give you insight into all this.
Allow him to minister alongside the parents.	**Philippians 2:22** But you know that Timothy has proved himself, because as a son with his father he has served with me in the work of the gospel.
Teach Him How to Deal With Those Who Have Money and Influence Teach him how to deal with people with monetary influence.	**1 Timothy 6:17-19** Command those who are rich in this present world not to be arrogant nor to put their hope in wealth, which is so uncertain, but to put their hope in God, who richly provides us with everything for our enjoyment. [18]Command them to do good, to be rich in good deeds, and to be generous and willing to share. [19]In this way they will lay up treasure for themselves as a firm foundation for the coming age, so that they may take hold of the life that is truly life.

Teach Him How to Deal With Those Who Pretend to be Religious Teach about those who pretend to be religious—sometimes those who make a show of being religious actually reject the things that would make them godly. Teach about who to associate with. Paul does not say to stay away from those who are not believers, but to avoid those who claim to believe, yet act otherwise.	Romans 10:2-3 For I can testify about them that they are zealous for God, but their zeal is not based on knowledge. ³Since they did not know the righteousness that comes from God and sought to establish their own, they did not submit to God's righteousness. 2 Timothy 3:2-9 People will be lovers of themselves, lovers of money, boastful, proud, abusive, disobedient to their parents, ungrateful, unholy, ³without love, unforgiving, slanderous, without self-control, brutal, not lovers of the good, ⁴treacherous, rash, conceited, lovers of pleasure rather than lovers of God— ⁵ having a form of godliness but denying its power. Have nothing to do with them. ⁶They are the kind who worm their way into homes and gain control over weak-willed women, who are loaded down with sins and are swayed by all kinds of evil desires, ⁷always learning but never able to acknowledge the truth. ⁸Just as Jannes and Jambres opposed Moses, so also these men oppose the truth—men of depraved minds, who, as far as the faith is concerned, are rejected. ⁹But they will not get

	very far because, as in the case of those men, their folly will be clear to everyone.
Let him know he may not be listened to, because people want to follow their own desires.	**2 Timothy 4:3-5** For the time will come when men will not put up with sound doctrine. Instead, to suit their own desires, they will gather around them a great number of teachers to say what their itching ears want to hear. ⁴They will turn their ears away from the truth and turn aside to myths. ⁵But you, keep your head in all situations, endure hardship, do the work of an evangelist, discharge all the duties of your ministry.
Teach about end times and the true nature of people.	**2 Timothy 3:1-4** But mark this: There will be terrible times in the last days. ²People will be lovers of themselves, lovers of money, boastful, proud, abusive, disobedient to their parents, ungrateful, unholy, ³without love, unforgiving, slanderous, without self-control, brutal, not lovers of the good, ⁴treacherous, rash, conceited, lovers of pleasure rather than lovers of God—
Discuss how to relate to others. He will not be able to	**1 Timothy 4:1-6** The Spirit clearly says that in

help everyone, but he must point out the truth.	latter times some will abandon the faith and follow deceiving spirits and things taught by demons. [2]Such teachings come through hypocritical liars, whose consciences have been seared as with a hot iron. [3]They forbid people to marry and order them to abstain from certain foods, which God created to be received with thanksgiving by those who believe and who know the truth. [4]For everything God created is good, and nothing is to be rejected if it is received with thanksgiving, [5]because it is consecrated by the word of God and prayer. [6]If you point these things out to the brothers, you will be a good minister of Christ Jesus, brought up in the truths of the faith and of the good teaching that you have followed.
Teach how to interact with those who oppose the parents.	1 Timothy 6:20-21 Timothy, guard what has been entrusted to your care. Turn away from godless chatter and the opposing ideas of what is falsely called knowledge, [21]which some have professed and in so doing have wandered from the faith. Grace be with you. 2 Timothy 1:8 So do not be ashamed to testify

	about our Lord, or ashamed of me, his prisoner. But join with me in suffering for the gospel, by the power of God,
Teach how to recognize unbelievers.	**2 Timothy 2:19** Nevertheless, God's solid foundation stands firm, sealed with this inscription: "The Lord knows those who are his," and, "Everyone who confesses the name of the Lord must turn away from wickedness." **1 Timothy 6:3-5** If anyone teaches false doctrines and does not agree to the sound instruction of our Lord Jesus Christ and to godly teaching, ⁴he is conceited and understands nothing. He has an unhealthy interest in controversies and quarrels about words that result in envy, strife, malicious talk, evil suspicions ⁵and constant friction between men of corrupt mind, who have been robbed of the truth and who think that godliness is a means to financial gain.
Remind Them Of Their Spiritual Journey Remind him of his spiritual journey, what he has been taught and who taught him.	**2 Timothy 3:13-15** while evil men and impostors will go from bad to worse, deceiving and being deceived. ¹⁴But as for you, continue in what you have learned and have

Paul reminds Timothy of his spiritual roots to encourage him in his gift and to encourage him to not be fearful and timid. Sometimes those who have grown up in the faith are seen as naïve by those who experienced a sinful life before they were saved.

Tell Him His Parents' Spiritual Journey

Be an example as a parent regarding what is taught, lifestyle, and motives. Let love and patient endurance serve as examples. Share life events so he can see how God worked—not just the fruit of His works.

Teach Values

Having an adequate value system enables believers to be useful to God.

become convinced of, because you know those from whom you learned it, [15]and how from infancy you have known the holy Scriptures, which are able to make you wise for salvation through faith in Christ Jesus.

2 Timothy 1:5
I have been reminded of your sincere faith, which first lived in your grandmother Lois and in your mother Eunice and, I am persuaded, now lives in you also.

2 Timothy 3:10-12
You, however, know all about my teaching, my way of life, my purpose, faith, patience, love, endurance, [11]persecutions, sufferings—what kinds of things happened to me in Antioch, Iconium and Lystra, the persecutions I endured. Yet the Lord rescued me from all of them. [12] In fact, everyone who wants to live a godly life in Christ Jesus will be persecuted,

2 Timothy 2:20-22
In a large house there are articles not only of gold and silver, but also of wood and clay; some are

for noble purposes and some for ignoble. ²¹If a man cleanses himself from the latter, he will be an instrument for noble purposes, made holy, useful to the Master and prepared to do any good work.

²²Flee the evil desires of youth, and pursue righteousness, faith, love and peace, along with those who call on the Lord out of a pure heart.

It is sometimes difficult for young people to realize life is not fair and that evil people and imposters will flourish, but Paul advises Timothy to do what is right, regardless of what others are doing.

2 Timothy 3:13-15

while evil men and impostors will go from bad to worse, deceiving and being deceived. ¹⁴But as for you, continue in what you have learned and have become convinced of, because you know those from whom you learned it, ¹⁵and how from infancy you have known the holy Scriptures, which are able to make you wise for salvation through faith in Christ Jesus.

Some good works will not be known by others until later, but good works cannot be hidden.

1 Timothy 5:24-25

The sins of some men are obvious, reaching the place of judgment ahead of them; the sins of others trail behind them. ²⁵In the same way, good deeds are obvious, and even those that are not cannot be hidden.

Teach respect. It is sometimes easier to be disrespectful and take advantage of those in authority when they are Christians.	1 Timothy 6:1-2 All who are under the yoke of slavery should consider their masters worthy of full respect, so that God's name and our teaching may not be slandered. ²Those who have believing masters are not to show less respect for them because they are brothers. Instead, they are to serve them even better, because those who benefit from their service are believers, and dear to them. These are the things you are to teach and urge on them.
Encourage him to cling to faith and have a clear conscience.	1 Timothy 1:18-19 Timothy, my son, I give you this instruction in keeping with the prophecies once made about you, so that by following them you may fight the good fight, ¹⁹holding on to faith and a good conscience. Some have rejected these and so have shipwrecked their faith.
Teach him to be devoted to reading, teaching, and preaching the Word; to use his gifts, be diligent, and persevere so he and his hearers will be saved.	1 Timothy 4:13-16 Until I come, devote yourself to the public reading of scripture, to preaching and to teaching. ¹⁴Do not neglect your gift, which was given you through a prophetic message when the body of elders laid their hands on you. ¹⁵Be diligent in these matters; give yourself wholly

to them, so that everyone may see your progress. [16]Watch your life and doctrine closely. Persevere in them, because if you do, you will save both yourself and your hearers

Teach him to flee evil, pursue righteousness, persevere, fight, hold, and obey. Paul could command Timothy to obey because he had a relationship with him.

1 Timothy 6:11-14

But you, man of God, flee from all this, and pursue righteousness, godliness, faith, love, endurance and gentleness. [12]Fight the good fight of the faith. Take hold of the eternal life to which you were called when you made your good confession in the presence of many witnesses. [13]In the sight of God, who gives life to everything, and of Christ Jesus, who while testifying before Pontius Pilate made the good confession, I charge you [14]to keep this command without spot or blame until the appearing of our Lord Jesus Christ,

2 Timothy 2:22

Flee the evil desires of youth, and pursue righteousness, faith, love and peace, along with those who call on the Lord out of a pure heart.

Teach how to perform self-analysis. This is a process of

1 Timothy 4:16

Watch your life and doctrine

being honest to self and being self-aware of one's short-comings.	closely. Persevere in them, because if you do, you will save both yourself and your hearers.
	1 Timothy 5:21-22 I charge you, in the sight of God and Christ Jesus and the elect angels, to keep these instructions without partiality, and to do nothing out of favoritism. [22]Do not be hasty in the laying on of hands, and do not share in the sins of others. Keep yourself pure.
Teach that God gives strength to endure suffering. Do not be ashamed of suffering for the gospel. This is not the same as suffering for wrong doing.	**2 Timothy 1:8** So do not be ashamed to testify about our Lord, or ashamed of me his prisoner. But join with me in suffering for the gospel, by the power of God,
	2 Timothy 2:3 Endure hardship with us like a good soldier of Christ Jesus.
	1 Peter 2:20 But how is it to your credit if you receive a beating for doing wrong and endure it? But if you suffer for doing good and you endure it, this is commendable before God.
Suffering brings an opportunity to develop and	**2 Timothy 1:7-8** For God did not give us a spirit

show power, love, and self-discipline.

of timidity, but a spirit of power, of love and of self–discipline. [8]So do not be ashamed to testify about our Lord, or ashamed of me his prisoner. But join with me in suffering for the gospel, by the power of God,

One reason for suffering is to bring salvation to others.

2 Timothy 2:9-10

for which I am suffering even to the point of being chained like a criminal. But God's word is not chained. [10]Therefore I endure everything for the sake of the elect, that they too may obtain the salvation that is in Christ Jesus, with eternal glory.

Teach The Spiritual Child What And How To Teach Others

Instruct on what to teach and how to remind others of basic truths.

2 Timothy 2:14

Keep reminding them of these things. Warn them before God against quarreling about words; it is of no value, and only ruins those who listen.

Perhaps Timothy enjoyed arguing too much, or perhaps it was just part of being young, but Paul warned him several times about this issue. Timothy may have still been learning how to use discernment. He may not have understood that what seemed evident to him as a course of action was not evident to others. Timothy may have

2 Timothy 2:23-26

Don't have anything to do with foolish and stupid arguments, because you know they produce quarrels. [24]And the Lord's servant must not quarrel; instead, he must be kind to everyone, able to teach, not resentful. [25]Those who oppose him he must gently instruct, in the hope that God will grant them repentance leading them viewed his discernment as common sense and therefore would have been upset when others did not understand what seemed so clear to him. Paul told him what *not* to do, in terms of being reactive (stop it, avoid it), and also how to be proactive (be kind to everyone, teach effectively, be patient with difficult people, gently teach) in order to get the desired results from God. If a child exhibits behavior that is causing concern, do not be afraid to keep dealing with it; however, it should be dealt with it in a comprehensive way. Give reasons for stopping the behavior, present alternative behaviors, and show how the results will be more beneficial when done God's way. Arguing leads people away from salvation. Kindness, effective and gentle teaching, and patience allows God to work. Ultimately it is God who must change their hearts.

Focus on the Word and its purpose. Focus on the divinity of Scripture and what it does: it teaches what is true, identifies problem areas, and provides solutions. The word teaches to do what is

to a knowledge of the truth, [26]and that they will come to their senses and escape from the trap of the devil, who has taken them captive to do his will.

2 Timothy 4:5
But you, keep your head in all situations, endure hardship, do the work of an evangelist, discharge all the duties of your ministry.

2 Timothy 3:16-17
All Scripture is God-breathed and is useful for teaching, rebuking, correcting and training in righteousness, [17]so that the man of God may be thoroughly equipped for every

right and equips for every good thing God desires to be accomplished.

Go over basic teachings again and again. Repetition is important for attachment disorder individuals due to cognitive distortion, in the same way as consistent caregiving reinforces attachment.

good work.

2 Timothy 2:11-13

Here is a trustworthy saying: If we died with him, we will also live with him; 12if we endure, we will also reign with him. If we disown him, he will also disown us; 13if we are faithless, he will remain faithful, for he cannot disown himself.

1 Timothy 2:3-6

This is good, and pleases God our Savior, 4who wants all men to be saved and to come to a knowledge of the truth. 5For there is one God and one mediator between God and men, the man Christ Jesus, 6who gave himself as a ransom for all men—the testimony given in its proper time.

1 Timothy 6:13-16

In the sight of God, who gives life to everything, and of Christ Jesus, who while testifying before Pontius Pilate made the good confession, I charge you 14to keep this command without spot or blame until the appearing of our Lord Jesus Christ, 15which God will bring about in his own time—God, the blessed and only Ruler, the King of kings and Lord of lords, [16]who alone is immortal and who lives in unapproachable light, whom no one has seen or can see. To him be honor and might forever. Amen.

2 Timothy 1:9-12

who has saved us and called us to a holy life—not because of anything we have done but because of his own purpose and grace. This grace was given us in Christ Jesus before the beginning of time, [10]but it has now been revealed through the appearing of our Savior, Christ Jesus, who has destroyed death and has brought life and immortality to light through the gospel. [11]And of this gospel I was appointed a herald and an apostle and a teacher. [12]That is why I am suffering as I am. Yet I am not ashamed, because I know whom I have believed, and am convinced that he is able to guard what I have entrusted to him for that day.

2 Timothy 2:8

Remember Jesus Christ, raised from the dead, descended from David. This is my gospel,

Teach manners.	1 Timothy 5:1-2 Do not rebuke an older man harshly, but exhort him as if he were your father. Treat younger men as brothers, ²older women as mothers, and younger women as sisters, with absolute purity.
Teach compassion, however, this compassion should not encourage codependency, entitlement, or assuming responsibility that belongs to others.	1 Timothy 5:3-11 Give proper recognition to those widows who are really in need. ⁴But if a widow has children or grandchildren, these should learn first of all to put their religion into practice by caring for their own family and so repaying their parents and grandparents, for this is pleasing to God. ⁵The widow who is really in need and left all alone puts her hope in God and continues night and day to pray and to ask God for help. ⁶But the widow who lives for pleasure is dead even while she lives. ⁷Give the people these instructions, too, so that no one may be open to blame. ⁸If anyone does not provide for his relatives, and especially for his immediate family, he has denied the faith and is worse than an unbeliever. ⁹No widow may be put on the list of widows unless she is over sixty, has been faithful to her husband, ¹⁰and is well known for her good deeds, such as

	bringing up children, showing hospitality, washing the feet of the saints, helping those in trouble and devoting herself to all kinds of good deeds. [11]As for younger widows, do not put them on such a list. For when their sensual desires overcome their dedication to Christ, they want to marry.
Teach the importance of family responsibilities.	1 Timothy 5:4 But if a widow has children or grandchildren, these should learn first of all to put their religion into practice by caring for their own family and so repaying their parents and grandparents, for this is pleasing to God.
Give instructions regarding appropriate behavior.	1 Timothy 2:9-10 I also want women to dress modestly, with decency and propriety, not with braided hair or gold or pearls or expensive clothes, [10]but with good deeds, appropriate for women who profess to worship God. 1 Timothy 4:12 Don't let anyone look down on you because you are young, but set an example for the believers in speech, in life, in love, in faith and in purity.

Give The Child Opportunities To Exercise Authority This giving of authority enables him to experience situations where he is responsible for others that are accountable to him as well as model the way giving of authority is passed on to others. Parents should be available to give advice, support, and feedback.	
Give the authority to command the end of inappropriate teaching.	1 Timothy 1:3-4 As I urged you when I went into Macedonia, stay there in Ephesus so that you may command certain men not to teach false doctrines any longer ⁴nor to devote themselves to myths and endless genealogies. These promote controversies rather than God's work—which is by faith.
Give the authority to set rules of behavior.	1 Timothy 3:14-15 Although I hope to come to you soon, I am writing you these instructions so that, ¹⁵if I am delayed, you will know how people ought to conduct themselves in God's household, which is the church of the living God, the pillar and foundation of the truth.

	2 Timothy 2:14 Keep reminding them of these things. Warn them before God against quarreling about words; it is of no value, and only ruins those who listen.
Give the authority to command, to teach, and to be an example for others.	1 Timothy 4:11-12 Command and teach these things. [12]Don't let anyone look down on you because you are young, but set an example for the believers in speech, in life, in love, in faith and in purity.
Give the authority to teach the truth and encourage obedience.	1 Timothy 6:2 Those who have believing masters are not to show less respect for them because they are brothers. Instead, they are to serve them even better, because those who benefit from their service are believers, and dear to them. These are the things you are to teach and urge on them.
Teach Administrative Skills Give instructions on how to be an administrator, how to determine who is reliable and qualified, and to delegate responsibilities.	2 Timothy 2:2 And the things you have heard me say in the presence of many witnesses entrust to reliable men who will also be qualified to teach others.
Teach about church leadership. Note that leadership focuses more on character than on	1 Timothy 3:1-2 Here is a trustworthy saying: If anyone sets his heart on being

management skills.	an overseer, he desires a noble task. [2]Now the overseer must be above reproach, the husband of but one wife, temperate, self-controlled, respectable, hospitable, able to teach,
	1 Timothy 3:8-9 Deacons, likewise, are to be men worthy of respect, sincere, not indulging in much wine, and not pursuing dishonest gain. [9]They must keep hold of the deep truths of the faith with a clear conscience.
	1 Timothy 3:11 In the same way, their wives are to be women worthy of respect, not malicious talkers but temperate and trustworthy in everything.
Teach how to manage and resolve conflict in a positive way.	**1 Timothy 5:19-20** Do not entertain an accusation against an elder unless it is brought by two or three witnesses. [20]Those who sin are to be rebuked publicly, so that the others may take warning.
Teach how to take time when appointing people for ministries.	**1 Timothy 5:22** Do not be hasty in the laying on of hands, and do not share in the sins of others. Keep yourself pure.

Teach About the Future **Tell of the prize that awaits**	2 Timothy 4:6-9 For I am already being poured out like a drink offering, and the time has come for my departure. [7]I have fought the good fight, I have finished the race, I have kept the faith. [8]Now there is in store for me the crown of righteousness, which the Lord, the righteous Judge, will award to me on that day—and not only to me, but also to all who have longed for his appearing. [9]Do your best to come to me quickly,
Teach About Prayer Pray for kings and authorities.	1 Timothy 2:1-2 I urge, then, first of all, that requests, prayers, intercession and thanksgiving be made for everyone— [2]for kings and all those in authority, that we may live peaceful and quiet lives in all godliness and holiness.
Pray without anger or disputes.	1 Timothy 2:8 I want men everywhere to lift up holy hands in prayer, without anger or disputing.
Reproduce Yourself Teach him how to be a parent.	2 Timothy 4:1-2 In the presence of God and of Christ Jesus, who will judge the living and the dead, and in view of his appearing and his kingdom, I give you this

	charge: [2]Preach the Word; be prepared in season and out of season; correct, rebuke and encourage—with great patience and careful instruction.
	2 Timothy 2:2 And the things you have heard me say in the presence of many witnesses entrust to reliable men who will also be qualified to teach others.

The primary way to empower children is through consistent care-giving behavior in the form of intercessory prayer, emotional nurturing, worshipping together, and teaching biblical truth. This process builds a foundation for a spiritual heritage and a reciprocal relationship with God, through Jesus Christ. This bond enables two individuals to develop a dynamic "covenant relationship." When a vacuum exists, something will fill it. If no parent is available, that need will be filled by a substitute. A child who lacks family will find substitutes in sports, hobbies, drugs, or gangs. A secure base attachment is the equivalent of having a stable and perpetual covenant relationship with God. When this covenant relationship is established, prayers and grace are released in new ways and come from the spirit instead of being limited by emotional needs. When a person is able to receive inner healing from an attachment disorder, he can establish many secure base attachment/covenant relationships.

Within the context of covenant relationship and with anointing from the Holy Spirit, "agreement in prayer" becomes truly possible. People with residual attachment disorder have profound difficulty agreeing with others. This falls under the concept of:

> **Matthew 12:25**
> Jesus knew their thoughts and said to them, "Every kingdom divided against itself will be ruined, and every city or household divided against itself will not stand."

Whereas those who are able to establish covenant relationships are able to function under:

> **Matthew 18:19**
> "Again, I tell you that if two of you on earth agree about anything you ask for, it will be done for you by my Father in heaven."

> **I Corinthians 1:10**
> I appeal to you, brothers, in the name of our Lord Jesus Christ, that all of you agree with one another so that there may be no divisions among you and that you may be perfectly united in mind and thought.

> **Colossians 3:16**
> Let the word of Christ dwell in you richly as you teach and admonish one another with all wisdom, and as you sing psalms, hymns and spiritual songs with gratitude in your hearts to God.

Inner healing from an attachment disorder typically is progressive rather than instantaneous. Jesus healed both instantaneously *and* progressively.

> **Mark 8:23-25**
> He took the blind man by the hand and led him outside the village. When he had spit on the man's eyes and put his hands on him, Jesus asked, "Do you see anything?" ²⁴He looked up and said, "I see people; they look like trees walking around." ²⁵Once more Jesus put his hands on the man's eyes. Then his eyes were opened, his sight was restored, and he saw everything clearly.

Luke 17:14
When he saw them, he said, "Go, show yourselves
to the priests." And as they went, they were
cleansed.

A relationship with a child may be troubled at the beginning.
Re-parenting coupled with intercessory prayer can help the child
mature and move with greater expediency toward the Heavenly
Father's love, grace, and faith.

I Corinthians 3:1-2
Brothers, I could not address you as spiritual but
as worldly—mere infants in Christ. I gave you
milk, not solid food, for you were not yet ready
for it. Indeed, you are still not ready.

Hebrews 5:12-13
In fact, though by this time you ought to be
teachers, you need someone to teach you the
elementary truths of God's word all over again.
You need milk, not solid food! [13]Anyone who lives
on milk, being still an infant, is not acquainted with
the teaching about righteousness.

I Peter 2:2
Like newborn babies, crave pure spiritual milk, so
that by it you may grow up in your salvation,

An example of covenant relationship/friendship can be seen in
the interaction between David and Jonathan. David was higher in
authority, being anointed by God to be the king, but Jonathan was
a parenting figure who provided support and nurturing to David.

I Samuel 18:3-4
And Jonathan made a covenant with David
because he loved him as himself. [4]Jonathan took
off the robe he was wearing and gave it to David,
along with his tunic, and even his sword, his bow
and his belt.

I Samuel 19:1-2
Saul told his son Jonathan and all the attendants
to kill David. But Jonathan was very fond of David
²and warned him, "My father Saul is looking for a
chance to kill you. Be on your guard tomorrow
morning; go into hiding and stay there.

I Samuel 20:16
So Jonathan made a covenant with the house of
David, saying, "May the Lord call David's enemies
to account."

Ruth and Naomi also established a covenant relationship.

Ruth 1:16
But Ruth replied, "Don't urge me to leave you or
to turn back from you. Where you go I will go,
and where you stay I will stay. Your people will be
my people and your God my God.

Jesus was never alone, which is indicative of someone who
values covenant relationship.

John 8:29
The one who sent me is with me; he has not left
me alone, for I always do what pleases him."

Scripture indicates the importance of relationships.

Genesis 2:18
The Lord God said, "It is not good for the man to
be alone. I will make a helper suitable for him."

John 14:18
I will not leave you as orphans; I will come to
you.

Hebrews 10:25
Let us not give up meeting together, as some are in the habit of doing, but let us encourage one another—and all the more as you see the Day approaching.

Acts 2:42
They devoted themselves to the apostles' teaching and to the fellowship, to the breaking of bread and to prayer.

1 John 1:7
But if we walk in the light, as he is in the light, we have fellowship with one another, and the blood of Jesus, his Son, purifies us from all sin.

These scriptural references reflect the importance of secure base attachment/covenant relationships between adults in the context of being a member of the family of God through our Lord and Savior Jesus Christ. Altruistic love is a significant part of interpersonal love relationships and religious love relationships contribute to more positive mental health.[46] Altruistic love is composed of many components that have been well studied in other contexts, including; maternal-child bonding, social interactions, positive/supportive behaviors (e.g., hand-holding), positive emotional states (happiness, pleasure, reward), and the placebo effect.

Studies have shown that isolated individuals—either lonely students or isolated ageing individuals in the inner city—show a threat pattern of heart rate variability and blood pressure response.[47] Social isolation and feelings of loneliness independently compromised the students' immune systems.[48] Therefore, positive interpersonal relationships can prop up day-to-day health.[49]

---

46 "Veterans battle emotional trauma with love," *Science & Theology News*, (June 2005).

47 J. T. Cacioppo, J. M. Ernst, M. H. Burleson, M. K. McClintock, W. B. Malarkey, L. C. Hawkley, R. B. Kowalewski, A. Paulsen, J. A. Hobson, K. Hugdahl, D. Spiegel and G. G. Berntson. "Lonely traits and concomitant physiological processes: The MacArthur social neuroscience studies," International Journal of Psychophysiology **35 (2000):** 143-54.

48 R. Adelson, "Only the lonely," *Monitor on Psychology*, 36 (May 2005): 26-27.

49 S. D. Pressman, S Cohen, G. E. Miller, A. Barkin, B. S. Rabin and J. J. Treanor. "Loneliness, social network size, and immune response to influenza vaccination in college freshmen." *Health Psychology* 24 (May 2005): 297-306.

Chapter 8

Covenants and Spiritual Adoption of Adults

Due to attachment disorders there are many adults that need spiritual re-parenting. Much of what is applicable to re-parenting an adopted child can be applied to parenting relationships between believers. Psychospiritual skills are learned through relationships with others. Within the relationship between the parent and the one being parented, it is necessary to develop a behavioral contract pursuing the following objectives in the process of developing a secure base attachment/covenant relationship.

COVENANT RELATIONSHIPS

COVENANTS REQUIRE MORE THAN ONE PARTY. **GOD'S PART OF THE COVENANT** God enters into a covenant with individuals with a solemn oath.	Ezekiel 16:8 " 'Later I passed by, and when I looked at you and saw that you were old enough for love, I spread the corner of my garment over you and covered your nakedness. I gave you my solemn oath and entered into a covenant with you, declares the Sovereign Lord, and you became mine.
God remembers the covenant for the sake of His children.	Psalm 106:44-45 But he took note of their distress when he heard their cry; [45]for their sake he remembered his

	covenant and out of his great love he relented.
His covenant will never fail.	Psalm 89:28 I will maintain my love to him forever, and my covenant with him will never fail.
	Isaiah 54:10 Though the mountains be shaken and the hills be removed, yet my unfailing love for you will not be shaken nor my covenant of peace be removed," says the Lord, who has compassion on you.
His covenant is everlasting.	Isaiah 55:3 Give ear and come to me; hear me, that your soul may live. I will make an everlasting covenant with you, my faithful love promised to David.
	Isaiah 61:8 "For I, the Lord, love justice; I hate robbery and iniquity. In my faithfulness I will reward them and make an everlasting covenant with them.
COVENANT REQUIRES MUTUAL RESPECT BETWEEN HUMAN BEINGS There is a willingness to	Proverbs 17:9 He who covers over an offense promotes love, but whoever repeats the matter separates close friends.

exercise self-control by withholding judgment or criticism and to learn how to be used by the Holy Spirit manifesting the gift of grace for mutual encouragement of spiritual growth to maturity.	1 Peter 4:8 Above all, love each other deeply, because love covers over a multitude of sins.
COVENANT REQUIRES SHARING	1 Samuel 18:3-4 And Jonathan made a covenant with David because he loved him as himself. ⁴Jonathan took off the robe he was wearing and gave it to David, along with his tunic, and even his sword, his bow and his belt.
COVENANT REQUIRES TRUST David trusted Jonathan's word that Saul would not kill him. David's ability to trust Jonathan is a reflection of his secure base attachment with his biological father, Jesse.	1 Samuel 19:6-7 Saul listened to Jonathan and took this oath: "As surely as the Lord lives, David will not be put to death." ⁷So Jonathan called David and told him the whole conversation. He brought him to Saul, and David was with Saul as before.
COVENANT REQUIRES VULNERABILITY There is a willingness to be transparent, vulnerable, and emotionally available for the sake of the relationship.	Philippians 2:5-8 Your attitude should be the same as that of Christ Jesus: ⁶Who, being in very nature God, did not consider equality with God something to be grasped, ⁷but made himself nothing, taking the very nature of a servant, being made in human likeness. ⁸And being

	found in appearance as a man, he humbled himself and became obedient to death—even death on a cross!
	Philippians 2:3 Do nothing out of selfish ambition or vain conceit, but in humility consider others better than yourselves.
COVENANT REQUIRES EXCLUSIVENESS The covenant excludes those who are not a part of the covenant.	Deuteronomy 7:9 Know therefore that the Lord your God is God; he is the faithful God, keeping his covenant of love to a thousand generations of those who love him and keep his commands.
	Psalm 42:8 By day the Lord directs his love, at night his song is with me—a prayer to the God of my life.
	Exodus 34:14 Do not worship any other god, for the Lord, whose name is Jealous, is a jealous God.
COVENANT REQUIRES PROTECTION	Psalm 40:11 Do not withhold your mercy from me, O Lord; may your love and your truth always protect me.

	Psalm 59:16
	But I will sing of your strength, in the morning I will sing of your love; for you are my fortress, my refuge in times of trouble.
	Psalm 60:5
	Save us and help us with your right hand, that those you love may be delivered.
COVENANT REQUIRES FAITHFULNESS	Nehemiah 9:17
	They refused to listen and failed to remember the miracles you performed among them. They became stiff-necked and in their rebellion appointed a leader in order to return to their slavery. But you are a forgiving God, gracious and compassionate, slow to anger and abounding in love. Therefore you did not desert them,
	Psalm 89:1-2
	A maskil of Ethan the Ezrahite. I will sing of the Lord's great love forever; with my mouth I will make your faithfulness known through all generations. ²I will declare that your love stands firm forever, that you established your faithfulness in heaven itself.

COVENANT REQUIRES HONESTY	2 Corinthians 4:2 Rather, we have renounced secret and shameful ways; we do not use deception, nor do we distort the word of God. On the contrary, by setting forth the truth plainly we commend ourselves to every man's conscience in the sight of God. Ephesians 4:15 Instead, speaking the truth in love, we will in all things grow up into him who is the Head, that is, Christ. 1 John 1:6 If we claim to have fellowship with him yet walk in the darkness, we lie and do not live by the truth.
COVENANT REQUIRES CONFIDENTIALITY	Ephesians 4:31 Get rid of all bitterness, rage and anger, brawling and slander, along with every form of malice. James 4:11 Brothers, do not slander one another. Anyone who speaks against his brother or judges him speaks against the law and judges it. When you judge the law, you are not keeping it, but sitting in judgment on it.

COVENANT REQUIRES PREPARATION A willingness to meditate on the written word (Logos).	Joshua 1:8 Do not let this Book of the Law depart from your mouth; meditate on it day and night, so that you may be careful to do everything written in it. Then you will be prosperous and successful. Psalm 48:9 Within your temple, O God, we meditate on your unfailing love. Psalm 119:99 I have more insight than all my teachers, for I meditate on your statutes.
Pray for Holy Spirit guidance.	Romans 8:27 And he who searches our hearts knows the mind of the Spirit, because the Spirit intercedes for the saints in accordance with God's will. Romans 12:2 Do not conform any longer to the pattern of this world, but be transformed by the renewing of your mind. Then you will be able to test and approve what God's will is—his good, pleasing and perfect will.

	James 1:5
	If any of you lacks wisdom, he should ask God, who gives generously to all without finding fault, and it will be given to him.
	Ephesians 6:18
	And pray in the Spirit on all occasions with all kinds of prayers and requests. With this in mind, be alert and always keep on praying for all the saints.
COVENANT REQUIRES REFLECTION	Lamentations 3:40
Reflection is the willingness to recognize the impact of generational sin (pathology) and the required commitment for continued psychospiritual growth to maturity.	Let us examine our ways and test them, and let us return to the Lord.
	2 Corinthians 13:5
	Examine yourselves to see whether you are in the faith; test yourselves. Do you not realize that Christ Jesus is in you—unless, of course, you fail the test?

Within the context of the covenant relationship, mutual respect and trust become possible whereby the two individuals can have the freedom to speak about differences of opinion without anticipatory fear of jeopardizing the relationship. The development of mutual respect and trust gives birth to empathy, compassion, and mercy. This individual will experience a sense of being reborn into a nurturing family, thereby released from a life of generational sin and a dysfunctional family system to secure base attachment relationship.

Adults with anxious ambivalent and avoidant attachment styles have a significantly higher number of relationship-specific irrational beliefs than those who have a secure base attachment. Relationship-specific irrational beliefs were associated with reduced relationship satisfaction for both sexes.[50] These irrational beliefs can include undependability and untrustworthiness due to cognitive distortion.

> I Corinthians 13:12
>
> Now we see but a poor reflection as in a mirror; then we shall see face to face. Now I know in part; then I shall know fully, even as I am fully known.

From a counseling perspective, a therapist may decide to use a secular technique, such as cognitive restructuring techniques to deal with distorted or irrational thinking. However, from a psychospiritual point of view, therapeutic prayer is preferable. Kosek,[51] Taylor, and MacDonald[52] indicate that "agreeableness and conscientiousness" positively correlate with religious involvement and religious orientation.

---

50 R. A. Staclert and K. Bursik, "Why am I unsatisfied? Adult attachment style, gendered irrational relationship beliefs, and young adult romantic relationship satisfaction," *Personality and Individual Differences* 34 (2003).

51 R. B. Kosek, "Adaptation of the big five as a hermeneutic instrument for religious constructs," *Personality and Individual Differences* 27 (1999).

52 A. Taylor and D. MacDonald, "Religion and the five factor model of personality: An exploratory investigation using a Canadian University sample," *Personality and Individual Differences* 27 (1999).

Agreeableness and Conscientiousness

Agreeableness	1 Corinthians 1:10 I appeal to you, brothers, in the name of our Lord Jesus Christ, that all of you agree with one another so that there may be no divisions among you and that you may be perfectly united in mind and thought. Philippians 4:2 I plead with Euodia and I plead with Syntyche to agree with each other in the Lord. 1 Corinthians 6:7 The very fact that you have lawsuits among you means you have been completely defeated already. Why not rather be wronged? Why not rather be cheated? Hebrews 12:14 Make every effort to live in peace with all men and to be holy; without holiness no one will see the Lord.
Conscientiousness	Proverbs 18:9 One who is slack in his work is brother to one who destroys. Matthew 7:12 So in everything, do to others

	what you would have them do to you, for this sums up the Law and the Prophets.
	1 Corinthians 15:58
	Therefore, my dear brothers, stand firm. Let nothing move you. Always give yourselves fully to the work of the Lord, because you know that your labor in the Lord is not in vain.
	Colossians 3:23
	Whatever you do, work at it with all your heart, as working for the Lord, not for men,
	1 Peter 4:10
	Each one should use whatever gift he has received to serve others, faithfully administering God's grace in its various forms.

Agreeableness and conscientiousness are traits not commonly associated with attachment disorder—quite the opposite in fact. However, it is possible for people with this disorder to develop an attitude of "agreeableness and conscientiousness" without therapy or prayer-based healing for the underlying problem. People with attachment disorders may develop a façade of psychospiritual stability, minimizing the consequences of their disorder. This does not reflect true psychospiritual personality changes through the process of psychospiritual formation and re-parenting.

We can only speculate through the life of Moses whether or not he truly had the opportunity to be re-parented. His father-in-law, Jethro, may have re-parented Moses as they were together a "long period of time" (Exod. 2:15-23). However, Jethro was not there to give input while Moses was parenting Israel.

Exodus 4:18-20

Then Moses went back to Jethro his father-in-law and said to him, "Let me go back to my own people in Egypt to see if any of them are still alive." Jethro said, "Go, and I wish you well." ¹⁹Now the Lord had said to Moses in Midian, "Go back to Egypt, for all the men who wanted to kill you are dead." ²⁰So Moses took his wife and sons, put them on a donkey and started back to Egypt. And he took the staff of God in his hand.

The re-parenting that may have taken place is evidenced by Jethro giving advice to Moses and Moses taking it.

Exodus 18:14-24

When his father-in-law saw all that Moses was doing for the people, he said, "What is this you are doing for the people? Why do you alone sit as judge, while all these people stand around you from morning till evening?" ¹⁵Moses answered him, "Because the people come to me to seek God's will. ¹⁶Whenever they have a dispute, it is brought to me, and I decide between the parties and inform them of God's decrees and laws." ¹⁷Moses' father-in-law replied, "What you are doing is not good. ¹⁸You and these people who come to you will only wear yourselves out. The work is too heavy for you; you cannot handle it alone. ¹⁹Listen now to me and I will give you some advice, and may God be with you. You must be the people's representative before God and bring their disputes to him. ²⁰Teach them the decrees and laws, and show them the way to live and the duties they are to perform. ²¹But select capable men from all the people—men who fear God,

trustworthy men who hate dishonest gain—
and appoint them as officials over thousands,
hundreds, fifties and tens. ²²Have them serve as
judges for the people at all times, but have them
bring every difficult case to you; the simple cases
they can decide themselves. That will make your
load lighter, because they will share it with you.
²³If you do this and God so commands, you will
be able to stand the strain, and all these people
will go home satisfied." ²⁴Moses listened to his
father-in-law and did everything he said.

However, Moses again sent his father-in-law away when
perhaps he should have kept him there for consultation.

Exodus 18:27

Then Moses sent his father-in-law on his way, and
Jethro returned to his own country.

Although he experienced psychospiritual transformation
directly from the Lord during his encounters with God, as well as
re-parenting from Jethro, Moses did not have the opportunity to
practice the knowledge that he gained. Consequently, he did not
know how to parent Israel.

Moses

Moses was abandoned/rejected over and over. When he was left in the Nile at three months of age, who knows how long his cries went unanswered? He was abandoned after being weaned. He was again abandoned by the Hebrews and Pharaoh when he killed the Egyptian. This multiple	Exodus 2:2-3 And she became pregnant and gave birth to a son. When she saw that he was a fine child, she hid him for three months. ³But when she could hide him no longer, she got a papyrus basket for him and coated it with tar and pitch. Then she placed the child in it and put it

sense of separation loss from consistent nurturing relationships had a cumulative effect on Moses' ambivalent attachment style. This hindered his ability to be agreeable with the great I AM in his initial interaction during the burning bush episode. His sense of agreeableness was repeatedly strained each time he did not see the expected result of Pharaoh releasing the Israelites.

among the reeds along the bank of the Nile.

Exodus 2:5-6

Then Pharaoh's daughter went down to the Nile to bathe, and her attendants were walking along the river bank. She saw the basket among the reeds and sent her slave girl to get it. [6]She opened it and saw the baby. He was crying, and she felt sorry for him. "This is one of the Hebrew babies," she said.

Exodus 2:8-9

"Yes, go," she answered. And the girl went and got the baby's mother. [9]Pharaoh's daughter said to her, "Take this baby and nurse him for me, and I will pay you." So the woman took the baby and nursed him.

Exodus 2:10

When the child grew older, she took him to Pharaoh's daughter and he became her son. She named him Moses, saying, "I drew him out of the water."

Exodus 2:15

When Pharaoh heard of this, he tried to kill Moses, but Moses fled from Pharaoh and went to live in Midian, where he sat down by a well.

	Exodus 2:14 The man said, "Who made you ruler and judge over us? Are you thinking of killing me as you killed the Egyptian?" Then Moses was afraid and thought, "What I did must have become known."
Moses tried to combine his ethnic background with his cultural background by trying to identify with the Hebrews while acting like Egyptian royalty. This illustrates the great need of the anxious ambivalent person to have a sense of belonging, a secure base attachment—not only in relationships, but also with their social/cultural identity.	Acts 7:22-28 Moses was educated in all the wisdom of the Egyptians and was powerful in speech and action. ²³"When Moses was forty years old, he decided to visit his fellow Israelites. ²⁴He saw one of them being mistreated by an Egyptian, so he went to his defense and avenged him by killing the Egyptian. ²⁵Moses thought that his own people would realize that God was using him to rescue them, but they did not. ²⁶The next day Moses came upon two Israelites who were fighting. He tried to reconcile them by saying, 'Men, you are brothers; why do you want to hurt each other?' ²⁷"But the man who was mistreating the other pushed Moses aside and said, 'Who made you ruler and judge over us? ²⁸Do you want to kill me as you killed the Egyptian yesterday?

	Exodus 2:11-14
	One day, after Moses had grown up, he went out to where his own people were and watched them at their hard labor. He saw an Egyptian beating a Hebrew, one of his own people. [12]Glancing this way and that and seeing no one, he killed the Egyptian and hid him in the sand. [13]The next day he went out and saw two Hebrews fighting. He asked the one in the wrong, "Why are you hitting your fellow Hebrew?" [14]The man said, "Who made you ruler and judge over us? Are you thinking of killing me as you killed the Egyptian?" Then Moses was afraid and thought, "What I did must have become known."
Moses did not identify with his wife's family; he did not feel a sense of belonging, because he had not yet been re-parented or transformed psychospiritually.	Acts 7:29
	When Moses heard this, he fled to Midian, where he settled as a foreigner and had two sons.
	Exodus 2:21-22
	Moses agreed to stay with the man, who gave his daughter Zipporah to Moses in marriage. [22]Zipporah gave birth to a son, and Moses named him Gershom, saying, "I have become an alien in a foreign land."

Moses stayed a long time with Jethro, his father-in-law, but even that was not enough to overcome his attachment disorder.	Exodus 2:23 During that long period, the king of Egypt died. The Israelites groaned in their slavery and cried out, and their cry for help because of their slavery went up to God. Acts 7:30 "After forty years had passed, an angel appeared to Moses in the flames of a burning bush in the desert near Mount Sinai.
God dealt with Moses directly. Even with direct contact with God, Moses did not feel accepted. This shows us that God can use believers, even if they do not have a secure base attachment.	Exodus 3:4 When the Lord saw that he had gone over to look, God called to him from within the bush, "Moses! Moses!" And Moses said, "Here I am." Exodus 3:11 But Moses said to God, "Who am I, that I should go to Pharaoh and bring the Israelites out of Egypt?" Acts 7:30-34 "After forty years had passed, an angel appeared to Moses in the flames of a burning bush in the desert near Mount Sinai. [31]When he saw this, he was amazed at the sight. As he went over to look more closely, he heard the Lord's voice: [32]'I am the God of your fathers, the

God of Abraham, Isaac and Jacob.' Moses trembled with fear and did not dare to look. ³³"Then the Lord said to him, 'Take off your sandals; the place where you are standing is holy ground. ³⁴I have indeed seen the oppression of my people in Egypt. I have heard their groaning and have come down to set them free. Now come, I will send you back to Egypt.'

People without a secure base attachment are reluctant to do what God asks of them.	Exodus 4:13 But Moses said, "O Lord, please send someone else to do it."
God knew of Moses' insecurity, which may be why He said that Aaron would be glad to see Moses. Nevertheless, God was not happy with Moses' response. Until the attachment disorder is psychospiritually healed, agreeableness within the context of obedience is not attainable on a consistent basis.	Exodus 4:14 Then the Lord's anger burned against Moses and he said, "What about your brother, Aaron the Levite? I know he can speak well. He is already on his way to meet you, and his heart will be glad when he sees you.
Moses still identified with the Hebrews. Cognitive awareness or psychological insight does not in itself equal spirituality.	Exodus 4:18 Then Moses went back to Jethro his father-in-law and said to him, "Let me go back to my own people in Egypt to see if any of them are still alive." Jethro said, "Go, and I wish you well."

Moses over-reacted to the Israelites' criticism. He still presented the traits and features of anxious ambivalent attachment. This lack of compassion and mercy kept Moses from mediating differences with his people.	Exodus 17:1-4 The whole Israelite community set out from the Desert of Sin, traveling from place to place as the Lord commanded. They camped at Rephidim, but there was no water for the people to drink. ²So they quarreled with Moses and said, "Give us water to drink." Moses replied, "Why do you quarrel with me? Why do you put the Lord to the test?" ³But the people were thirsty for water there, and they grumbled against Moses. They said, "Why did you bring us up out of Egypt to make us and our children and livestock die of thirst?" ⁴Then Moses cried out to the Lord, "What am I to do with these people? They are almost ready to stone me."
Moses' parenting relationship with the Israelites was not one of love, but of strife. He saw himself as alone in keeping the Israelites in line. He was not fostering independence among the Israelites but dependency.	Numbers 20:10 He and Aaron gathered the assembly together in front of the rock and Moses said to them, "Listen, you rebels, must we bring you water out of this rock?" Deuteronomy 31:27-29 For I know how rebellious and stiff-necked you are. If you have been rebellious against the Lord while I am still alive and with you, how much more will you rebel after I die!

	[28]Assemble before me all the elders of your tribes and all your officials, so that I can speak these words in their hearing and call heaven and earth to testify against them. [29]For I know that after my death you are sure to become utterly corrupt and to turn from the way I have commanded you. In days to come, disaster will fall upon you because you will do evil in the sight of the Lord and provoke him to anger by what your hands have made."

Ineffective parenting has severe emotional, spiritual, and physical repercussions. Data indicates that ineffective parenting impacts the brain itself, affecting the neurochemistry of emotions and behavior. Preliminary research data shows evidence of a neurochemical basis of attachment, which the cited research articles refer to as pair bonding.[53, 54, 55] Among four neurochemicals identified for attachment thus far are: dopamine, vasopressin, oxytocin, and corticosterone. The references are provided for those who wish to pursue learning more about this topic.

The sequela of psycho/neuro and biochemical changes within the brain are the equivalent of generational sin. When ministering to people who have attachment disorders, there needs to be re-parenting and, equally important, divine physical healing.

53 Y. Liu, J. T. Curtis and Z. Wang, "Vasopressin in the lateral septum regulates pair bond formation in male prairie voles (Microtus orchrogaster)," *Behavioral Neurosciences* 115 (2001).

54 M.M. Cho, A.C. DeVries, J. R. Williams and C. S. Carter, "The effects of oxytocin and vasopressin on partner preferences in male and female prairie voles (Microtus ochrogaster)," *Behavioral Neuroscience* 113 (1999).

55 A.C. DeVries, M. B. DeVries, S.E. Taymans and C. S. Carter, "The effects of stress on social preferences are sexually dimorphic in prairie voles," *Proceedings of the National Academy of Sciences, USA* 93 (1996).

Chapter 9

Developing Trust

Developmental stages and skills relate to psychological and spiritual development. How children's needs and natural development are responded to determine how they respond to their parents and to others. This in turn establishes how they will respond to God. The adopted child must know that his adopted parent will not abandon him or leave him, in order to understand that God will not abandon him or leave him an orphan.

> Romans 8:35-39
>
> Who shall separate us from the love of Christ? Shall trouble or hardship or persecution or famine or nakedness or danger or sword? [36]As it is written: "For your sake we face death all day long; we are considered as sheep to be slaughtered." [37]No, in all these things we are more than conquerors through him who loved us. [38]For I am convinced that neither death nor life, neither angels nor demons, neither the present nor the future, nor any powers, [39]neither height nor depth, nor anything else in all creation, will be able to separate us from the love of God that is in Christ Jesus our Lord.

> John 14:18
>
> I will not leave you as orphans; I will come to you.

The developmental stages in language include both verbal and nonverbal communication. From birth infants recognize and prefer their mother's voice.[56] This ability to recognize the voice of the person who is most important in meeting their needs is the foundation for the ability to be able to identify the voice of God as the one who will meet their needs.

> Exodus 19:9
>
> The Lord said to Moses, "I am going to come to you in a dense cloud, so that the people will hear me speaking with you and will always put their trust in you." Then Moses told the Lord what the people had said.

The infant is responsive to sound and voices which is the basis for the person who has developed a trust relationship to be responsive to God, both to His voice and His written word. This responsiveness is mandatory for having an interactive prayer life as well as obedience. Trust and obedience go hand in hand.

> Exodus 24:7
>
> Then he took the Book of the Covenant and read it to the people. They responded, "We will do everything the Lord has said; we will obey."

> Deuteronomy 9:23
>
> And when the Lord sent you out from Kadesh Barnea, he said, "Go up and take possession of the land I have given you." But you rebelled against the command of the Lord your God. You did not trust him or obey him.

---

56 A. J. DeCasper and W. P. Fifer, "Of human bonding: Newborns prefer their mothers' voices," *Science, New Series* 208 (June 1980): 1174-76.

Deuteronomy 13:4

It is the Lord your God you must follow, and him you must revere. Keep his commands and obey him; serve him and hold fast to him.

Psalm 17:6

I call on you, O God, for you will answer me; give ear to me and hear my prayer.

Psalm 38:15

I wait for you, O Lord; you will answer, O Lord my God.

As an infant develops he is able to identify family members when he hears their name. This interaction enables the person with the ability to trust to extend beyond interacting with their mother and extend it to interacting with other family members and eventually those outside the family unit. This would be reflected in a person being able to fellowship within his family and then extend his relationships to other believers and develop relationships with unbelievers as well.

Acts 2:42

They devoted themselves to the apostles' teaching and to the fellowship, to the breaking of bread and to prayer.

1 Corinthians 1:9

God, who has called you into fellowship with his Son Jesus Christ our Lord, is faithful.

I John 1:3

We proclaim to you what we have seen and heard, so that you also may have fellowship with us. And our fellowship is with the Father and with his Son, Jesus Christ.

I Corinthians 5:9-11

I have written you in my letter not to associate with sexually immoral people— [10]not at all meaning the people of this world who are immoral, or the greedy and swindlers, or idolaters. In that case you would have to leave this world. [11]But now I am writing you that you must not associate with anyone who calls himself a brother but is sexually immoral or greedy, an idolater or a slanderer, a drunkard or a swindler. With such a man do not even eat.

In order for children to develop trust, their needs must be met. The adoptive parent must understand the development of his own trust within his family as well as his development of trust in God. This is important so that he can not only model the appropriate behavior but also provide teaching. To learn to trust God, believers must allow Him to meet their needs, be comforted by Him, and respond to His voice. In order to do this they must spend time talking to Him, listening to Him, reading His word, and believing and acting on what He says.

Biblical Precepts On Trust

TRUST	Psalm 9:10
God will never forsake those who seek Him.	Those who know your name will trust in you, for you, Lord, have never forsaken those who seek you.
Trust brings rejoicing.	Psalm 13:5 But I trust in your unfailing love; my heart rejoices in your salvation.
Trust in God, not things or plans.	Psalm 20:7 Some trust in chariots and some in horses, but we trust in the name of the Lord our God.
Trust brings victory.	Psalm 44:6-8 I do not trust in my bow, my sword does not bring me victory; [7]but you give us victory over our enemies, you put our adversaries to shame. [8]In God we make our boast all day long, and we will praise your name forever. Selah
The fundamental ability to trust comes when basic needs are met in infancy.	Psalm 22:9 Yet you brought me out of the womb; you made me trust in you even at my mother's breast.
Trust brings action, doing good. Trust in God will make the righteousness and the justice of an individual's cause known.	Psalm 37:3-6 Trust in the Lord and do good; dwell in the land and enjoy safe pasture. [4]Delight yourself in the Lord and he will give you the desires of your heart. [5]Commit

	your way to the Lord; trust in him and he will do this: ⁶He will make your righteousness shine like the dawn, the justice of your cause like the noonday sun.
Trust brings blessings.	Psalm 40:4 Blessed is the man who makes the Lord his trust, who does not look to the proud, to those who turn aside to false gods.
Trust removes fear of man; the response to fear should be trust.	Psalm 56:3-4 When I am afraid, I will trust in you. ⁴In God, whose word I praise, in God I trust; I will not be afraid. What can mortal man do to me? Psalm 56:11 in God I trust; I will not be afraid. What can man do to me?
Trust is continual. Trust is the ability to confide in God.	Psalm 62:8 Trust in him at all times, O people; pour out your hearts to him, for God is our refuge. Selah
Trust is a result of reverence for God.	Psalm 115:11 You who fear him, trust in the Lord—he is their help and shield.
Trust in God is better than trusting men even of high regard.	Psalm 118:8-9 It is better to take refuge in the Lord than to trust in man. ⁹It is better to take refuge in the Lord

	than to trust in princes.
Trust brings eternal life.	Psalm 125:1 A song of ascents. Those who trust in the Lord are like Mount Zion, which cannot be shaken but endures forever.
Trust allows God to speak to individuals and give them direction.	Psalm 143:8 Let the morning bring me word of your unfailing love, for I have put my trust in you. Show me the way I should go, for to you I lift up my soul.
Teaching brings trust in God.	Proverbs 22:19 So that your trust may be in the Lord, I teach you today, even you.
Trust brings salvation, strength, and worship.	Isaiah 12:2 Surely God is my salvation; I will trust and not be afraid. The Lord, the Lord, is my strength and my song; he has become my salvation." Isaiah 30:15 This is what the Sovereign Lord, the Holy One of Israel, says: "In repentance and rest is your salvation, in quietness and trust is your strength, but you would have none of it.
Trust brings joy, peace, and overflowing hope.	John 14:1 "Do not let your hearts be troubled. Trust in God; trust

	also in me.
	Romans 15:13 May the God of hope fill you with all joy and peace as you trust in him, so that you may overflow with hope by the power of the Holy Spirit.
The ability to trust God and people is interrelated. The ability to trust in a person is directly related to the ability to trust God.	**Exodus 19:9** The Lord said to Moses, "I am going to come to you in a dense cloud, so that the people will hear me speaking with you and will always put their trust in you." Then Moses told the Lord what the people had said.
	1 John 4:20 If anyone says, "I love God," yet hates his brother, he is a liar. For anyone who does not love his brother, whom he has seen, cannot love God, whom he has not seen.
Obedience and trust are interrelated.	**Psalm 78:7** Then they would put their trust in God and would not forget his deeds but would keep his commands.
Correction and discipline will not be accepted without trust.	**Zephaniah 3:1-2** Woe to the city of oppressors, rebellious and defiled! [2]She obeys no one, she accepts no correction. She does not trust in the Lord, she does not draw near to her God.

In order to develop trust with a child the adoptive parent must begin with the same developmental stages an infant goes through. First the parent needs to meet the child's basic physical and emotional needs such as food, clothing, kindness, love, compassion, and touch. This will develop into a relationship where the child will prefer the input of the adoptive parent to that of others, he will listen to that person and not be overwhelmed by listening to everyone.

John 10:27

My sheep listen to my voice; I know them, and they follow me.

Colossians 2:2-4

My purpose is that they may be encouraged in heart and united in love, so that they may have the full riches of complete understanding, in order that they may know the mystery of God, namely, Christ, [3]in whom are hidden all the treasures of wisdom and knowledge. [4]I tell you this so that no one may deceive you by fine-sounding arguments.

The child will be able to receive emotional and physical comfort from the adoptive parent. He will become responsive to their input and seeks them out, enjoys their company, begins to be aware of the local body of Christ, and then the worldwide body of Christ.

Without a secure base attachment rooted in trust the adopted child will not be able to receive from God. The absence of trust manifests as follows: the child who does not make the connection between his mother's voice and his needs being met will not have a foundation on which to develop a trust relationship with God or others. The lack of trust can manifest as disobedience.

Biblical Precepts On The Absence Of Trust

Unable to receive from God.	Numbers 20:12 But the Lord said to Moses and Aaron, "Because you did not trust in me enough to honor me as holy in the sight of the Israelites, you will not bring this community into the land I give them."
Refusal to listen and being prideful is a lack of trust.	2 Kings 17:14 But they would not listen and were as stiff–necked as their fathers, who did not trust in the Lord their God.
Putting trust in the wrong thing is unfaithfulness.	Job 31:24-28 "If I have put my trust in gold or said to pure gold, 'You are my security,'[25]if I have rejoiced over my great wealth, the fortune my hands had gained, [26]if I have regarded the sun in its radiance or the moon moving in splendor, [27]so that my heart was secretly enticed and my hand offered them a kiss of homage, [28]then these also would be sins to be judged, for I would have been unfaithful to God on high.
Lack of trust brings death.	Psalm 49:13-15 This is the fate of those who trust in themselves, and of their followers, who approve their sayings. *Selah* [14]Like sheep they are destined for the grave, and death will feed on them. The upright will rule over them in the morning; their forms will decay in the grave, far from

	their princely mansions. [15]But God will redeem my life from the grave; he will surely take me to himself.
There is judgment for lack of trust.	Psalm 62:10-12 Do not trust in extortion or take pride in stolen goods; though your riches increase, do not set your heart on them. [11]One thing God has spoken, two things have I heard: that you, O God, are strong, [12]and that you, O Lord, are loving. Surely you will reward each person according to what he has done.
Speaking against God is lack of trust. Not believing in God is lack of trust. Lack of trust makes God angry.	Psalm 78:19-22 They spoke against God, saying, "Can God spread a table in the desert? [20]When he struck the rock, water gushed out, and streams flowed abundantly. But can he also give us food? Can he supply meat for his people?" [21]When the LORD heard them, he was very angry; his fire broke out against Jacob, and his wrath rose against Israel, [22]for they did not believe in God or trust in his deliverance.
People value what they trust. People become like what they trust.	Psalm 115:3-8 Our God is in heaven; he does whatever pleases him. [4]But their idols are silver and gold, made by the hands of men. [5]They have mouths, but cannot speak, eyes, but they cannot see; [6]they have ears, but cannot hear, noses, but they cannot smell; [7]they have

	hands, but cannot feel, feet, but they cannot walk; nor can they utter a sound with their throats. ⁸Those who make them will be like them, and so will all who trust in them.
Misplaced trust keeps people from salvation.	Psalm 146:3 Do not put your trust in princes, in mortal men, who cannot save.
Lack of trust brings woe.	Isaiah 31:1 Woe to those who go down to Egypt for help, who rely on horses, who trust in the multitude of their chariots and in the great strength of their horsemen, but do not look to the Holy One of Israel, or seek help from the Lord.
Just because something is heard repeatedly does not mean it is trustworthy.	Jeremiah 7:4 Do not trust in deceptive words and say, "This is the temple of the Lord, the temple of the Lord, the temple of the Lord!"
Misplaced trust brings captivity.	Jeremiah 48:7 Since you trust in your deeds and riches, you too will be taken captive, and Chemosh will go into exile, together with his priests and officials.
Lack of trust brings disobedience and unwillingness to be teachable. Lack of trust keeps us from being close to God.	Zephaniah 3:2 She obeys no one, she accepts no correction. She does not trust in the Lord, she does not draw near to her God.

Chapter 10

The Physical, Psychological, and Spiritual Development of Obedience and Disobedience

An infant physically matures without any significant liabilities if he is provided with adequate physical nurturance such as touch, food, and shelter. Whereas psychological developmental growth requires consistency in physical and emotional parenting efforts in order to preclude attachment disorders. Development of obedience to authority tends to be contingent on the quality of care-taking the child experiences during the developmental and formative years.

As the child grows, and begins to establish a sense of autonomy and independence, he explores the limits of his psychological independence by "testing the limit" of adult authority. A typical toddler looks at the parent immediately prior to touching or doing something that is prohibited. The purpose of displaying oppositional behavior is to develop an independent sense of self; to proceed from oppositional behavior, to independence, self-discipline, and self-control. The primary function of oppositionality is to learn from experience what the boundaries of acceptable behavior are via feedback from the parent. When the parent ignores the oppositional behavior or is inconsistent in correcting unacceptable oppositional behavior, the child is unable to ascertain when and what is appropriate conduct.

In order for children to learn obedience, parents need to set an example by showing obedience to those in authority. Parents should be aware of how behavior and attitudes are passed on to their children. They should obey out of love and respect not out of fear of consequences and seek the Scriptures on what and why they are to be obedient.

There is a parallel development of physical, psychological, and spiritual maturity in the sequences of obedience, self-control, and self-discipline. From nine to twenty-four months the young child begins to assert himself. He goes from obedience to parents and those in authority to the "no" stage. The self-control/obedience he is developing at this time is dependent on external positive or negative consequences. This provides the foundation of obedience to God because of external consequences. As the child begins to desire independence he is still impulsive. He realizes that there are rules and obeys them without regard to the consequences but does not understand the reason behind the rules. This correlates with the new believer obeying God because of the "rule" as opposed to obedience because of the consequence. The progression of development then moves to the child actively seeking to learn the rules. They desire to know what is expected and they want to obey. Spiritually this provides the foundation of the desire to obey God and to seek out His rules. Lastly, the child begins to understand that rules provide protection they are not just to thwart the child's will. In the same way as the believer matures he will come to understand that God's rules are based in love, not to prevent pleasure, but to provide protection.

The advantages of obedience are clearly stated in Scripture; bringing benefits to the believer, their descendents, those in authority over them, and all nations, encompassing physical, spiritual, and emotional benefits.

Biblical Precepts On Obedience

Obedience leads to righteousness.	Romans 6:16 Don't you know that when you offer yourselves to someone to obey him as slaves, you are slaves to the one whom you obey—whether you are slaves to sin, which leads to death, or to obedience, which leads to righteousness?

Obedience brings well-being and enjoyment of long life.	Ephesians 6:1-3 Children, obey your parents in the Lord, for this is right.[2] "Honor your father and mother"—which is the first commandment with a promise—[3] "that it may go well with you and that you may enjoy long life on the earth."
Obedience pleases the Lord.	Colossians 3:20 Children, obey your parents in everything, for this pleases the Lord.
Obedience brings life.	Leviticus 18:4-5 You must obey my laws and be careful to follow my decrees. I am the Lord your God. [5]Keep my decrees and laws, for the man who obeys them will live by them. I am the Lord.
Obedience brings generational blessings and blessings to other nations.	Genesis 22:18 "And through your offspring all nations on earth will be blessed, because you have obeyed me.
Obedience enables possession of God's gifts.	Deuteronomy 4:1-2 Hear now, O Israel, the decrees and laws I am about to teach you. Follow them so that you may live and may go in and take possession of the land that the Lord, the God of your fathers, is giving you. [2]Do not

	add to what I command you and do not subtract from it, but keep the commands of the Lord your God that I give you.
Obedience brings joy to those in authority and is advantageous to the person who is obedient.	Hebrews 13:17 Obey your leaders and submit to their authority. They keep watch over you as men who must give an account. Obey them so that their work will be a joy, not a burden, for that would be of no advantage to you.
Obedience will be seen as wisdom and understanding by others, providing a good reputation among unbelievers.	Deuteronomy 4:6 Observe them carefully, for this will show your wisdom and understanding to the nations, who will hear about all these decrees and say, "Surely this great nation is a wise and understanding people."
Obedience brings the ability to teach children and grandchildren.	Deuteronomy 4:9 Only be careful, and watch yourselves closely so that you do not forget the things your eyes have seen or let them slip from your heart as long as you live. Teach them to your children and to their children after them.
Obedience brings generational blessings of long life to individuals and their children.	Deuteronomy 4:40 Keep his decrees and commands, which I am giving you today, so that it may go

	well with you and your children after you and that you may live long in the land the Lord your God gives you for all time.
Obedience brings God's love to an individual's descendants to a thousand generations.	Deuteronomy 5:10 but showing love to a thousand generations of those who love me and keep my commandments.
Obedience brings an excellent reputation. Obedience brings great assurance in faith in Jesus.	1 Timothy 3:13 Those who have served well gain an excellent standing and great assurance in their faith in Christ Jesus.
Obedience brings humility. Jesus humbled Himself; His obedience brought salvation. Obedience prevents selfishness and pride.	Philippians 2:5-8 Your attitude should be the same as that of Christ Jesus: 6Who, being in very nature God, did not consider equality with God something to be grasped, 7but made himself nothing, taking the very nature of a servant, being made in human likeness. 8And being found in appearance as a man, he humbled himself and became obedient to death—even death on a cross! John 6:38 For I have come down from heaven not to do my will but to do the will of him who sent me.

Obedience is evidence of authentic love. It brings a revelation of who Christ is and brings closeness to God and Jesus.	John 14:15 "If you love me, you will obey what I command. John 14:21 Whoever has my commands and obeys them, he is the one who loves me. He who loves me will be loved by my Father, and I too will love him and show myself to him." John 14:23 Jesus replied, "If anyone loves me, he will obey my teaching. My Father will love him, and we will come to him and make our home with him.
Obedience means remaining in Jesus' love.	John 15:10 If you obey my commands, you will remain in my love, just as I have obeyed my Father's commands and remain in his love.
Obedience means friendship with Jesus, not servitude.	John 15:14-15 You are my friends if you do what I command. [15]I no longer call you servants, because a servant does not know his master's business. Instead, I have called you friends, for everything that I learned from my Father I have made known to you.

When the parent is inconsistent in parenting responsibilities, the child experiences anticipatory anxiety typically manifesting as a form of conduct disorder such as disobedience to expected acceptable behavior. This disobedience is projected anger due to the sense of being abandoned, neglected, or ignored. Unmet physical and psychological needs are precursors to psychological maladjustments. When the nine to twenty-four month old child begins to assert himself has not been trained to be obedient, it inhibits the ability of the development of self-discipline. The lack of self-discipline and inability to be obedient makes spiritual maturity almost unattainable.

Biblical Precepts on Disobedience

DISOBEDIENCE	Jeremiah 48:10
Disobedience is not being diligent. Disobedience brings a curse.	"A curse on him who is lax in doing the LORD's work! A curse on him who keeps his sword from bloodshed!
Disobedience is doing things out of God's timing.	Numbers 14:39-45
	When Moses reported this to all the Israelites, they mourned bitterly. ⁴⁰Early the next morning they went up toward the high hill country. "We have sinned," they said. "We will go up to the place the LORD promised." ⁴¹But Moses said, "Why are you disobeying the LORD's command? This will not succeed! ⁴²Do not go up, because the LORD is not with you. You will be defeated by your enemies, ⁴³for the Amalekites and Canaanites will face you there. Because you have turned away from the LORD, he will not be with

you and you will fall by the sword." ⁴⁴Nevertheless, in their presumption they went up toward the high hill country, though neither Moses nor the ark of the LORD's covenant moved from the camp. ⁴⁵Then the Amalekites and Canaanites who lived in that hill country came down and attacked them and beat them down all the way to Hormah.

Disobedience is obtaining God's gifts out of God's timing

Matthew 4:1-11

Then Jesus was led by the Spirit into the desert to be tempted by the devil. ²After fasting forty days and forty nights, he was hungry. ³The tempter came to him and said, "If you are the Son of God, tell these stones to become bread." ⁴Jesus answered, "It is written: 'Man does not live on bread alone, but on every word that comes from the mouth of God.'" ⁵Then the devil took him to the holy city and had him stand on the highest point of the temple. ⁶"If you are the Son of God," he said, "throw yourself down. For it is written: '"He will command his angels concerning you, and they will lift you up in their hands, so that you will not strike your foot against a stone.'" ⁷Jesus answered him, "It is also written: 'Do not put the Lord your God to the test.'" ⁸Again, the devil took him to a very high mountain and showed

	him all the kingdoms of the world and their splendor. [9]"All this I will give you," he said, "if you will bow down and worship me." [10]Jesus said to him, "Away from me, Satan! For it is written: 'Worship the Lord your God, and serve him only.'" [11]Then the devil left him, and angels came and attended him.
There are punishments for disobedience.	Leviticus 26:14-41 " 'But if you will not listen to me and carry out all these commands, [15]and if you reject my decrees and abhor my laws and fail to carry out all my commands and so violate my covenant, [16]then I will do this to you: I will bring upon you sudden terror, wasting diseases and fever that will destroy your sight and drain away your life. You will plant seed in vain, because your enemies will eat it. [17]I will set my face against you so that you will be defeated by your enemies; those who hate you will rule over you, and you will flee even when no one is pursuing you. [18]" 'If after all this you will not listen to me, I will punish you for your sins seven times over. [19]I will break down your stubborn pride and make the sky above you like iron and the ground beneath you like bronze. [20]Your strength will be spent in vain, because your soil will not yield its crops, nor

will the trees of the land yield their fruit. [21]"'If you remain hostile toward me and refuse to listen to me, I will multiply your afflictions seven times over, as your sins deserve. [22]I will send wild animals against you, and they will rob you of your children, destroy your cattle and make you so few in number that your roads will be deserted. [23]" 'If in spite of these things you do not accept my correction but continue to be hostile toward me, [24]I myself will be hostile toward you and will afflict you for your sins seven times over. [25]And I will bring the sword upon you to avenge the breaking of the covenant. When you withdraw into your cities, I will send a plague among you, and you will be given into enemy hands. [26]When I cut off your supply of bread, ten women will be able to bake your bread in one oven, and they will dole out the bread by weight. You will eat, but you will not be satisfied. [27]" 'If in spite of this you still do not listen to me but continue to be hostile toward me, [28]then in my anger I will be hostile toward you, and I myself will punish you for your sins seven times over. [29]You will eat the flesh of your sons and the flesh of your daughters. [30]I will destroy your high places, cut down your incense altars and pile your dead bodies on the lifeless forms of your idols, and I will abhor you. [31]I will turn your cities into ruins and lay waste your sanctuaries, and I will take no delight in the pleasing aroma of your offerings. [32]I will lay waste the land, so that your enemies who live there will be appalled. [33]I will scatter you among the nations and will draw out my sword and pursue you. Your land will be laid waste, and your cities will lie in ruins. [34]Then the land will enjoy its sabbath years all the time that it lies desolate and you are in the country of your enemies; then the land will rest and enjoy its sabbaths. [35]All the time that it lies desolate, the land will have the rest it did not have during the sabbaths you lived in it. [36]"As for those of you who are left, I will make their hearts so fearful in the lands of their enemies that the sound of a windblown leaf will put them to flight. They will run as though fleeing from the sword, and they will fall, even though no one is pursuing them. [37]They will stumble over one another as though fleeing from the sword, even though no one is pursuing them. So you will not be able to stand before your enemies. [38]You will perish among the nations; the land of your enemies will devour you. [39]Those of you who are left will waste away in the lands of their enemies because of their sins; also because of their fathers' sins they will waste away. [40]" 'But if they will confess their sins and the sins of their fathers—their treachery against me and their hostility toward me, [41]which made me hostile toward them so that I sent them into the land of their enemies—then when their uncircumcised hearts are humbled and they pay for their sin,

The consequences of disobedience negatively affects up to the third and fourth generations. However, those generations are not accountable for the sin of their forefathers, only for the sins they personally commit. The sins of forefathers must not be used to negate personal culpability.

Deuteronomy 5:9
You shall not bow down to them or worship them; for I, the LORD your God, am a jealous God, punishing the children for the sin of the fathers to the third and fourth generation of those who hate me,

Ezekiel 18:2-3
"What do you people mean by quoting this proverb about the land of Israel: " 'The fathers eat sour grapes, and the children's teeth are set on edge'? [3]"As surely as I live, declares the Sovereign Lord, you will no longer quote this proverb in Israel.

Disobedience prevents salvation.

Hebrews 2:2-3
For if the message spoken by angels was binding, and every violation and disobedience received its just punishment,

	[3]how shall we escape if we ignore such a great salvation? This salvation, which was first announced by the Lord, was confirmed to us by those who heard him.
Disobedience excludes us from God's rest.	**Hebrews 4:6** It still remains that some will enter that rest, and those who formerly had the gospel preached to them did not go in, because of their disobedience.
Disobedience causes others to fall.	**Hebrews 4:11** Let us, therefore, make every effort to enter that rest, so that no one will fall by following their example of disobedience.
Disobedience brings great disaster.	**Jeremiah 43:1-45:5** **Jeremiah 44:10-11** "To this day they have not humbled themselves or shown reverence, nor have they followed my law and the decrees I set before you and your fathers. [11]"Therefore, this is what the Lord Almighty, the God of Israel, says: I am determined to bring disaster on you and to destroy all Judah.
Disobedience is lack of love.	**John 14:24** He who does not love me will not obey my teaching. These words you hear are not my own; they belong to the Father who sent me.

Secure base attachment is the primary foundation for healthy obedience. One of the most powerful means of encouraging or discouraging a specific behavior is through reward or punishment. Parental attitudes and values have a considerable significance in determining which behavior is rewarded or punished. An authentically autonomous and independent act of obedience is contingent on whether the decision to comply is based on fear of punishment or positive awareness of the outcome of the desired behavior. It is contingent on the developmental age of the child, i.e., a toddler may obey a parent out of conditioned response to the authority figure without cognitive awareness as to the outcome of such behavior. As the child matures the covenant relational responsibilities become operational in the decision to be obedient or not. John states, "We love because He first loved us" (1 John 4:19). The loving and nurturing relationship between parent and child is influential in the cognitive decision making due process of whether to be obedient or not. Healthy obedience, in contrast to obedience based on fear and intimidation, is foundational of secure base attachments and nurturing relationships. Obedience based on trust relationships is what is typically referred to as covenant relationship. As noted in the book of Deuteronomy the people were encouraged to never forget the gracious God who gave them the land nor their responsibilities to worship Him with the correct attitude. Children who are provided with a secure base attachment will remember with affection their relational interaction with their parents and will maintain an attitude of compassion and gratitude. The "Deuteronomist called for right worship at the right time in the right place,"[57] This is the message of Deuteronomy 6:4-19.

> **Deuteronomy 6:4-5**
> Hear, O Israel: The LORD our God, the LORD is one. [5]Love the LORD your God with all your heart and with all your soul and with all your strength.

Compliance to this mandate is the biblical illustration of healthy obedience.

---

57 Jacob M. Meyers, "The Requisites for Response," *Interpretation* 15 (1961): 21.

Chapter 11

The Foundations of a Healthy Relationship

Before a person can form healthy relationships with others, it is necessary to have a good self-concept. That includes an understanding of who he is in Christ and the fact that God created each person and He chose them. The foundation of a good self-concept is secure base attachment; the foundation of a good self-image is the realization that he is made in God's image. It is important for the adoptive parent to have a healthy concept of how much he is loved by God so that they can impart that same love to their adopted child.

Belonging To God

He chose you before the creation of the world.	Ephesians 1:4-8
He chose you to be holy and blameless in His sight.	For he chose us in him before the creation of the world to be holy and blameless in his sight.
It was His pleasure to choose you.	In love [5]he predestined us to be adopted as his sons through Jesus Christ, in accordance with
He gave you His grace freely and lavishly in Christ.	his pleasure and will— [6]to the praise of his glorious grace,
He gave you redemption.	which he has freely given us in the One he loves. [7]In him we
He gave you forgiveness of sins.	have redemption through his blood, the forgiveness of sins, in accordance with the riches of God's grace [8]that he lavished on us with all wisdom and understanding.

He delights in you.	Psalm 147:11 The Lord delights in those who fear him, who put their hope in his unfailing love.
God desires your love.	Matthew 22:37-38 Jesus replied: "'Love the Lord your God with all your heart and with all your soul and with all your mind.' [38]This is the first and greatest commandment.
You are the righteousness of God.	2 Corinthians 5:21 God made him who had no sin to be sin for us, so that in him we might become the righteousness of God.
You are wonderfully made. To reject your personality, giftings, or body is to reject something God has made for you. You are rejecting His gift.	Psalm 139:14 I praise you because I am fearfully and wonderfully made; your works are wonderful, I know that full well. Colossians 1:4 **(AMP)** For we have heard of your faith in Christ Jesus [the leaning of your entire human personality on Him in absolute trust and confidence in His power, wisdom, and goodness] and of the love which you [have and show] for all the saints (God's consecrated ones),

	Psalm 33:15 He who forms the hearts of all, who considers everything they do.
	Ephesians 2:10 For we are God's workmanship, created in Christ Jesus to do good works, which God prepared in advance for us to do.
The part that is to be made new is lifestyle and beliefs, not the physical body. The promise of a new body comes in the resurrection.	Ephesians 4:22-24 You were taught, with regard to your former way of life, to put off your old self, which is being corrupted by its deceitful desires; [23]to be made new in the attitude of your minds; [24]and to put on the new self, created to be like God in true righteousness and holiness.
	1 Corinthians 15:42 So will it be with the resurrection of the dead. The body that is sown is perishable, it is raised imperishable;
You are to rejoice in how God made you.	1 Timothy 4:4 For everything God created is good, and nothing is to be rejected if it is received with thanksgiving,
You are to recognize that God made you, He is in control.	Acts 4:24 When they heard this, they

	raised their voices together in prayer to God. "Sovereign Lord," they said, "you made the heaven and the earth and the sea, and everything in them.
	Acts 17:28-30 'For in him we live and move and have our being.' As some of your own poets have said, 'We are his offspring.' [29]"Therefore since we are God's offspring, we should not think that the divine being is like gold or silver or stone—an image made by man's design and skill. [30]In the past God overlooked such ignorance, but now he commands all people everywhere to repent.

Unless a believer grasps the fact that he was created by God to match God's standard of beauty, the believer will never fully trust God. God's ultimate intention is for His children to experience perfection through redemption, regeneration, and eventually transformation. Due to consequences of sinful nature, aggravated by inappropriate or inconsistent parenting patterns, individuals tend to have multiple liabilities that preclude being able to receive God's ultimate intention for their lives. Identity in Christ is the primary vehicle of self-acceptance.

The following enumerated concepts dispel common misbeliefs of believers who struggle with consequences of attachment disorders.

1. Holiness in Christ does not mean we must be perfect. Mistakes are not intentional sin.

Psalm 139:23-24

Search me, O God, and know my heart; test me and know my anxious thoughts. [24]See if there is any offensive way in me, and lead me in the way everlasting.

Psalm 130:3-4

If you, O Lord, kept a record of sins, O Lord, who could stand? [4]But with you there is forgiveness; therefore you are feared

2. Emotional acceptance means having the right to feel hurt and the right to feel angry. What an individual chooses to do with his emotions is the issue. The counsel of "people can't hurt you, only you can allow them to hurt you" perpetuates self-victimization. This concept is unbiblical. An abused, abandoned, or neglected child has the right to feel hurt. Paul experienced conflicts, fear, and depression. Those who care for the hurting will experience sorrow in their concern for the child. Heal the hurt and re-parent him to wholeness and spiritual maturity.

2 Corinthians 7:5-7

For when we came into Macedonia, this body of ours had no rest, but we were harassed at every turn—conflicts on the outside, fears within. [6]But God, who comforts the downcast, comforted us by the coming of Titus, [7]and not only by his coming but also by the comfort you had given him. He told us about your longing for me, your deep sorrow, your ardent concern for me, so that my joy was greater than ever.

Ephesians 4:26

"In your anger do not sin:" Do not let the sun go down while you are still angry,

3. Self-awareness in Christ means being aware of what God thinks of you as opposed to what man thinks of you.

Proverbs 29:25
Fear of man will prove to be a snare, but whoever trusts in the Lord is kept safe.

4. Pursuit of material goods as a substitute for emotional nurturance tends to be a behavior pattern for those individuals who suffer from anxious ambivalent attachment disorder due to fear of anticipatory rejection or anticipatory fear of failed relationships. Material goods invested in ministry effort are a blessing to the whole body of believers. Being able to share significant amounts of acquired possessions requires a sense of good self-image manifesting as benevolence.

Hebrews 13:5
Keep your lives free from the love of money and be content with what you have, because God has said, "Never will I leave you; never will I forsake you."

2 Corinthians 9:11
You will be made rich in every way so that you can be generous on every occasion, and through us your generosity will result in thanksgiving to God.

1 Timothy 6:17-18
Command those who are rich in this present world not to be arrogant nor to put their hope in wealth, which is so uncertain, but to put their hope in God, who richly provides us with everything for our enjoyment. [18]Command them

to do good, to be rich in good deeds, and to be generous and willing to share.

Philippians 4:11-12

I am not saying this because I am in need, for I have learned to be content whatever the circumstances. [12]I know what it is to be in need, and I know what it is to have plenty. I have learned the secret of being content in any and every situation, whether well fed or hungry, whether living in plenty or in want.

5.   Making decisions in Christ means eliminating false guilt or false fear imposed by yourself or others. Samuel was being obedient to God when he anointed Saul as king, he even warned the Israelites of the consequences, yet he grieved when Saul's disobedience caused him to be rejected as king by God. This was false guilt.

I Samuel 8:6-14

But when they said, "Give us a king to lead us," this displeased Samuel; so he prayed to the Lord. [7]And the Lord told him: "Listen to all that the people are saying to you; it is not you they have rejected, but they have rejected me as their king. [8]As they have done from the day I brought them up out of Egypt until this day, forsaking me and serving other gods, so they are doing to you. [9]Now listen to them; but warn them solemnly and let them know what the king who will reign over them will do." [10]Samuel told all the words of the Lord to the people who were asking him for a king. [11]He said, "This is what the king who will reign over you will do: He will take your sons and make them serve with his chariots and horses, and they will run in front of his chariots. [12]Some he will assign to be commanders of thousands and commanders of fifties, and others to plow his ground and reap his harvest, and still others to make weapons of war and equipment for his chariots. ¹³He will take your daughters to be perfumers and cooks and bakers. ¹⁴He will take the best of your fields and vineyards and olive groves and give them to his attendants.

I Samuel 8:21-22

When Samuel heard all that the people said, he repeated it before the Lord. ²²The Lord answered, "Listen to them and give them a king." Then Samuel said to the men of Israel, "Everyone go back to his town."

I Samuel 15:35-16:1

Until the day Samuel died, he did not go to see Saul again, though Samuel mourned for him. And the Lord was grieved that he had made Saul king over Israel. [16:1] The Lord said to Samuel, "How long will you mourn for Saul, since I have rejected him as king over Israel? Fill your horn with oil and be on your way; I am sending you to Jesse of Bethlehem. I have chosen one of his sons to be king."

Psalm 27:1

The Lord is my light and my salvation—whom shall I fear? The Lord is the stronghold of my life—of whom shall I be afraid?

To know one's identity in Christ enables the believer to have a foundation based not on a false self-concept but on truth based in God's word. This foundation will provide the ability to recognize areas that really need to be changed without feeling devastated or rejected.

Chapter 12

Psychospiritual Re-parenting

In light of the significant shortage of well trained Christian counselors and psychotherapists in the field of attachment therapy, psychospiritual re-parenting is the most efficacious and viable mode of intervention and rehabilitation for those who suffer from the consequences of attachment disorders. A study presented by psychologist Renee Soencer states that: "Decades of research have linked having one good relationship with an adult with all sorts of good outcomes for adolescents, but I was struck by how much of a role emotional support played in these relationships." [58] Soencer studied young men who lacked a father figure and were enrolled in the Big Brother program. The results indicate that having a relationship with a male mentor helps adolescent boys learn to reach out to others for support during stressful events.

This study is important to the idea of parenting children who have lacked family support. This study indicates that a child having just one meaningful relationship in their life will help them learn to reach out to others during times of distress. By implication, this would make them more receptive to the gospel and more teachable, especially if this information came from a parent who provided a secure base attachment. This secure base attachment can be seen as being "rooted in love."

---

58 A. Palmer, "Boy's emotional development addressed," *Monitor on Psychology* (October 2003).

Ephesians 3:16-19

I pray that out of his glorious riches he may strengthen you with power through his Spirit in your inner being, [17]so that Christ may dwell in your hearts through faith. And I pray that you, being rooted and established in love, [18]may have power, together with all the saints, to grasp how wide and long and high and deep is the love of Christ, [19]and to know this love that surpasses knowledge—that you may be filled to the measure of all the fullness of God.

Colossians 2:2-3

My purpose is that they may be encouraged in heart and united in love, so that they may have the full riches of complete understanding, in order that they may know the mystery of God, namely, Christ, [3]in whom are hidden all the treasures of wisdom and knowledge.

Attachment is the primary goal of parenting and re-parenting. Everything else is built on that foundation. It is imperative that parents realize this is their primary goal. As attachment and trust are developed, a strong, secure relationship develops. It is an ongoing process that occurs when the child's physical need for food, shelter, and touch, and the emotional need for compassion, encouragement, and unconditional love are met. Without that foundation, the parent-child relationship is based on fear of punishment, fear of abandonment, and fear of not having physical needs met. It becomes a conditional relationship.

In a mentoring relationship the person being mentored has the responsibility to initiate contact with their mentor. This is not true of spiritual adoption. With the spiritual adopted child it is the parent's responsibility to initiate contact and respond appropriately.

Re-parenting

To re-parent: Use object lessons.	Matthew 6:25-30 "Therefore I tell you, do not worry about your life, what you will eat or drink; or about your body, what you will wear. Is not life more important than food, and the body more important than clothes? [26]Look at the birds of the air; they do not sow or reap or store away in barns, and yet your heavenly Father feeds them. Are you not much more valuable than they? [27]Who of you by worrying can add a single hour to his life? [28]"And why do you worry about clothes? See how the lilies of the field grow. They do not labor or spin. [29]Yet I tell you that not even Solomon in all his splendor was dressed like one of these. [30]If that is how God clothes the grass of the field, which is here today and tomorrow is thrown into the fire, will he not much more clothe you, O you of little faith?
Take a difficult problem and simplify it so the solution can easily be seen.	Luke 18:1 Then Jesus told his disciples a parable to show them that they should always pray and not give up. Luke 18:5 yet because this widow keeps bothering me, I will see that

	she gets justice, so that she won't eventually wear me out with her coming!'"
Invite the child into the family's daily life. Let him participate in daily activities such as cooking, cleaning, and play. Do not treat him like company.	**Acts 2:46** Every day they continued to meet together in the temple courts. They broke bread in their homes and ate together with glad and sincere hearts, **1 Thessalonians 2:8** We loved you so much that we were delighted to share with you not only the gospel of God but our lives as well, because you had become so dear to us.

Improving this horizontal relationship with family members will form a strong foundation for developing a better vertical relationship with God. A vibrant and mature spiritual life is vital for psychological growth and essential for coping with the demands of daily living. Numerous research publications suggest that vibrant spirituality and religious fellowship tend to lessen psychological disorders and physical illness.

People around the world use prayer to cope with psychological distress although as mentioned previously those who are avoidant, avoid prayer.[59] A 1993 Gallup Poll cited by McCullough and Carson[60] states that 90 percent of North Americans pray at least occasionally. Empirical research on the

---

59 K. R. Byrd, and A. Boe, "The correspondence between attachment dimensions and prayer in college students," *International Journal for the Psychology of Religion* 11 (2001).

60 *Integrating spirituality into treatment: Resource for practitioners*, ed. W. R. Miller (Washington, D.C.: American Psychological Association, 1999).

effects of intercessory prayer on health has been criticized on the basis of methodological problems.[61] Nevertheless, research in this field suggests a positive impact of intercessory prayer. The following citations are a few of the positive results of prayer.

- The growth rate of bacteria was influenced by what scientists call "conscious intention."[62] Christians refer to this as intercessory prayer.

- The growth of cancerous tumors in laboratory animals was successfully reduced by laying on of hands.[63]

- Dermal wounds healed faster when treated by healers.[64]

- Healers had a success rate of 75.7 percent of wound closure in treatment groups as opposed to the success rate of 41.9 percent in control groups.[65]

Maximizing the protective influence of vibrant, mature spirituality requires a willingness to acknowledge negative experiences. Internalized emotions such as fear, anxiety, rage, and neurotic guilt as a consequence of an attachment disorder tend to hinder progress toward mature spirituality. Inappropriate parenting is addressed in Scripture.

61 L. Dorsey. *Healing words: The power of prayer and the practice of medicine* (New York: Harper Collins, 1993).

62 C. Nash, "Psychokinetic control of bacterial growth," *Journal of American Society of Psychical Research*, 51 (1982): 217-21.

63 B. Grad, "Healing by the laying on of hands: review of experiments and implications," *Pastoral Psychology*, 21(1970): 19-26.

64 B. Grad, R. Cadoret, and G. Paul, "The influence of an orthodox method of treatment on wound healing in mice," *International Journal of Parapsychology*, 3 (1961): 5-24.

65 L. D'Andrea-Winslow, D. Johnson, and A. Novitski, 2008, "Bioelectromagnetic energy fields accelerate wound healing and activate immune cell function," *Journal of Medical and Biological Sciences*, 2 (2008): 1-15.

Matthew 7:9-11

"Which of you, if his son asks for bread, will give him a stone? [10]Or if he asks for a fish, will give him a snake? [11]If you, then, though you are evil, know how to give good gifts to your children, how much more will your Father in heaven give good gifts to those who ask him!

Luke 6:36

Be merciful, just as your Father is merciful.

Ephesians 6:4

Fathers, do not exasperate your children; instead, bring them up in the training and instruction of the Lord.

Colossians 3:21

Fathers, do not embitter your children, or they will become discouraged.

1 Thessalonians 2:11-13

For you know that we dealt with each of you as a father deals with his own children, [12]encouraging, comforting and urging you to live lives worthy of God, who calls you into his kingdom and glory. [13]And we also thank God continually because, when you received the word of God, which you heard from us, you accepted it not as the word of men, but as it actually is, the word of God, which is at work in you who believe.

Hebrews 12:5-11

And you have forgotten that word of encouragement that addresses you as sons: "My son, do not make light of the Lord's discipline, and do not lose heart when he rebukes you,

⁶because the Lord disciplines those he loves, and he punishes everyone he accepts as a son." ⁷Endure hardship as discipline; God is treating you as sons. For what son is not disciplined by his father? ⁸If you are not disciplined (and everyone undergoes discipline), then you are illegitimate children and not true sons. ⁹Moreover, we have all had human fathers who disciplined us and we respected them for it. How much more should we submit to the Father of our spirits and live! ¹⁰Our fathers disciplined us for a little while as they thought best; but God disciplines us for our good, that we may share in his holiness. ¹¹No discipline seems pleasant at the time, but painful. Later on, however, it produces a harvest of righteousness and peace for those who have been trained by it.

I John 3:1

How great is the love the Father has lavished on us, that we should be called children of God! And that is what we are! The reason the world does not know us is that it did not know him.

Eliminating the consequences of "generational sin," due to inadequate or inappropriate parenting, demands the implementation of "identification repentance." This is a process of identifying with a group of individuals, entity, or family lineage and asking for forgiveness on their behalf.[66]

With greater spiritual awareness and psychological insight, the individual now is able to articulate in prayer his psychological dilemma that would make the process of "identification repentance" possible. One example of this concept is in Nehemiah 1:6, whereby Nehemiah prayed to the

---

66 For a more thorough discussion of this concept see J. Dawson *Taking Our Cities For God* (Lake Mary, Florida: Charisma House 2001) and *Releasing Destiny: A Spiritual Warfare Manual for Nashville and Country Music*, ed. S. Mansfield (Nashville: Daniel 1 School of Leadership, 1993) 49-52.

Lord, "I confess the sins we Israelites, including myself and my father's house, have committed against you."

The main objective of re-parenting children is to help them overcome the attachment disorder that hinders their vertical relationship with God and their horizontal relationships with others. Overcoming the attachment dysfunction allows a dynamic and reciprocal nurturing fellowship within the body of believers, which is kononia.

Chapter 13

Faith and Attachment Style

Faith, in Greek, is *pisteos*:

> to win over, persuade.... Subjectively meaning firm persuasion, conviction, belief in the truth, veracity, reality or faithfulness (though rare). Objectively meaning that which is believed, doctrine, the received articles of faith... In Hebrews 11:1... means that persuasion is not the outcome of imagination but is based on fact, such as the reality of the resurrection of Christ (1 Cor. 15), and as such it becomes the basis of realistic hope.... In 2 Corinthians 5:7... means that which appears before us may not be what it seems to be, whole faith is something which stands on proof arrived at inductively.[67]

Faith means embracing the uncertainty of hope and desire. For the secure base attachment person, this is not a major problem. Such people have the capacity to allow faith to dwell in themselves.

> I Peter I:8
>
> Though you have not seen him, you love him; and even though you do not see him now, you believe in him and are filled with an inexpressible and glorious joy,

---

67 S. Zodhiates, *The Complete Word Study Dictionary New Testament* (Chattanooga, TN: AMG International, Inc, 1993): 1162.

By contrast, people with insecure attachment place a high value on control. Therefore, they lack the ability to live by faith. Living in faith means giving up control, or the illusion of control, which would evoke disabling anxiety. The insecurely attached person may have the intellectual ability to commit the Word to memory, but is unable to let the logos become part of himself. This person's experience demands physical and tangible evidence, which is the opposite of faith. This individual needs to see and hear in order to believe. This brings to mind Thomas, the doubting disciple. Although there is no data regarding Thomas' parents, he provides a good example of insecure attached faith.

John 20:24-29

Now Thomas (called Didymus), one of the Twelve, was not with the disciples when Jesus came. [25]So the other disciples told him, "We have seen the Lord!" But he said to them, "Unless I see the nail marks in his hands and put my finger where the nails were, and put my hand into his side, I will not believe it." [26]A week later his disciples were in the house again, and Thomas was with them. Though the doors were locked, Jesus came and stood among them and said, "Peace be with you!" [27]Then he said to Thomas, "Put your finger here; see my hands. Reach out your hand and put it into my side. Stop doubting and believe." [28]Thomas said to him, "My Lord and my God!" [29]Then Jesus told him, "Because you have seen me, you have believed; blessed are those who have not seen and yet have believed."

Many Christians hunger for visible and verifiable miracles because of their experience with insecure attachment. They always need assurance. Without signs and wonders, they are unable to mature in their faith.

John 4:48

"Unless you people see miraculous signs and wonders," Jesus told him, "you will never believe."

John 6:2

and a great crowd of people followed him because they saw the miraculous signs he had performed on the sick.

John 12:37

Even after Jesus had done all these miraculous signs in their presence, they still would not believe in him.

This is the reflection of the American lifestyle and/or the "latchkey children" syndrome. After a short maternity leave, anywhere from two weeks to two months, working mothers take their infant to a daycare provider. Time spent with the infant is minimal. As the child grows older, extra curricular activities above and beyond their academic responsibilities minimize nurturing family interaction and inhibit secure base attachment.

People with insecure attachment have tremendous unfulfilled needs; therefore their lives are based primarily on meeting physical and emotional needs, to the detriment of spiritual things. When they try to exist in the spiritual dimension, they experience psychological distress and revert to feelings of abandonment.

Naomi provides an excellent model of someone who re-parented an adult.

Naomi and Ruth

Naomi's husband Elimelech was a good provider, and she followed him. A secure base attached person has a greater capacity for submission.	Ruth 1:1 In the days when the judges ruled, there was a famine in the land, and a man from Bethlehem in Judah, together with his wife and two sons, went to live for a while in the country of Moab.
Naomi's sons, Mahlon and Kilon followed their father's example as providers and took care of Naomi until they died. Securely attached parents have a greater capacity to perpetuate generational blessings.	Ruth 1:3-5 Now Elimelech, Naomi's husband, died, and she was left with her two sons. ⁴They married Moabite women, one named Orpah and the other Ruth. After they had lived there about ten years, ⁵both Mahlon and Kilion also died, and Naomi was left without her two sons and her husband.
Naomi was willing to let her daughter-in-laws return to their own mothers. She had developed a close relationship with them, and they wept when she gave them a blessing and kissed them goodbye. Naomi was willing to allow them to make their own decisions. Naomi was an adoptive parent to Orpah and Ruth.	Ruth 1:6-9 When she heard in Moab that the Lord had come to the aid of his people by providing food for them, Naomi and her daughters-in-law prepared to return home from there. ⁷With her two daughters-in-law she left the place where she had been living and set out on the road that would take them back to the land of Judah. ⁸Then Naomi said to her two daughters-in-law, "Go back, each of you, to your mother's home. May the Lord show kindness to you, as

Although Naomi encouraged Ruth to go back to her mother as Orpah did, once she knew Ruth had made up her mind to stay, she stopped questioning her about the decision. Once an adult child has made a decision, we decision they should be allowed to follow it.

Ruth made a commitment to be Naomi's daughter. This reflected Naomi's successful effort to re-parent Ruth, thereby establishing a secure base attachment with her.

Ruth submitted to Naomi's authority, even though she was taking care of Naomi's needs. She asked permission from Naomi to go and glean the fields. Ruth placed herself under the authority of the foreman by asking permission to glean. These are

you have shown to your dead and to me. [9]May the Lord grant that each of you will find rest in the home of another husband." Then she kissed them and they wept aloud

Ruth 1:17-18

Where you die I will die, and there I will be buried. May the Lord deal with me, be it ever so severely, if anything but death separates you and me." [18]When Naomi realized that Ruth was determined to go with her, she stopped urging her.

Ruth 1:16-17

But Ruth replied, "Don't urge me to leave you or to turn back from you. Where you go I will go, and where you stay I will stay. Your people will be my people and your God my God. [17]Where you die I will die, and there I will be buried. May the Lord deal with me, be it ever so severely, if anything but death separates you and me."

Ruth 2:2

And Ruth the Moabitess said to Naomi, "Let me go to the fields and pick up the leftover grain behind anyone in whose eyes I find favor." Naomi said to her, "Go ahead, my daughter."

illustrations of a secure base attached individual who has the capacity to submit.

Ruth 2:6-7

The foreman replied, "She is the Moabitess who came back from Moab with Naomi. [7]She said, 'Please let me glean and gather among the sheaves behind the harvesters.' She went into the field and has worked steadily from morning till now, except for a short rest in the shelter."

Ruth 2:17

So Ruth gleaned in the field until evening. Then she threshed the barley she had gathered, and it amounted to about an ephah.

A person with a secure base attached relationship is able to be truly grateful and make themselves vulnerable to the kindness of others. They do not have a sense of entitlement.

Ruth 2:10

At this, she bowed down with her face to the ground. She exclaimed, "Why have I found such favor in your eyes that you notice me—a foreigner?"

As a daughter, Ruth was committed to Naomi with love and kindness. She left her own family and her religion. A person adopted as an adult may have to give up family, religion, lifestyle, and friends when they make a commitment to their adoptive parent.

Ruth 2:11

Boaz replied, "I've been told all about what you have done for your mother-in-law since the death of your husband—how you left your father and mother and your homeland and came to live with a people you did not know before.

Ruth not only gave Naomi the grain, she shared her lunch. A secure base individual is capable of being self-sacrificial, thereby fulfilling the mandate of loving their neighbor as themselves.

Naomi demonstrated that although Ruth did the work, they should be thankful for the person who helped her and ask God to bless him. Ruth shared with Naomi the opportunities that were before her and sought her council. As an adoptive parent, Naomi was continually teaching.

Ruth 2:18

She carried it back to town, and her mother-in-law saw how much she had gathered. Ruth also brought out and gave her what she had left over after she had eaten enough.

Ruth 2:19-20

Her mother-in-law asked her, "Where did you glean today? Where did you work? Blessed be the man who took notice of you!" Then Ruth told her mother-in-law about the one at whose place she had been working. "The name of the man I worked with today is Boaz," she said. [20]"The Lord bless him!" Naomi said to her daughter-in-law. "He has not stopped showing his kindness to the living and the dead." She added, "That man is our close relative; he is one of our kinsman-redeemers."

Ruth 2:21-23

Then Ruth the Moabitess said, "He even said to me, 'Stay with my workers until they finish harvesting all my grain.'" [22]Naomi said to Ruth her daughter-in-law, "It will be good for you, my daughter, to go with his girls, because in someone else's field you might be harmed." [23]So Ruth stayed close to the servant girls of Boaz to glean until the barley and wheat harvests were finished. And she lived with her mother-in-law.

Possibly Ruth could have chosen to stay with the field hands, but instead chose to stay with her adoptive mother. This is the second time Ruth chose to put her adoptive mother's needs above her own. This is how parenting should continue. First the parent cares for the child; then the child cares for the parent. However, the parent should not depend on their child financially but instead for assistance in things they are no longer physically or mentally able to do.

Even though Ruth was an adult, Naomi still guided her, and Ruth obeyed Naomi. This is another illustration of the responsibility of the adoptive parent to continue teaching if the secure child manifests continued willingness to be taught.

Ruth 2:23

So Ruth stayed close to the servant girls of Boaz to glean until the barley and wheat harvests were finished. And she lived with her mother–in–law.

2 Corinthians 12:14

Now I am ready to visit you for the third time, and I will not be a burden to you, because what I want is not your possessions but you. After all, children should not have to save up for their parents, but parents for their children.

Ruth 3:1-6

One day Naomi her mother-in-law said to her, "My daughter, should I not try to find a home for you, where you will be well provided for? [2]Is not Boaz, with whose servant girls you have been, a kinsman of ours? Tonight he will be winnowing barley on the threshing floor. [3]Wash and perfume yourself, and put on your best clothes. Then go down to the threshing floor, but don't let him know you are there until he has finished eating and drinking. [4]When he lies down, note the place where he is lying. Then go and uncover his feet and lie down. He will tell you what to do." [5]"I will do whatever you say," Ruth answered. [6]So she went down to the threshing floor and did everything her mother-in-law told her to do.

Ruth shared personal experiences with Naomi, and Naomi encouraged her to be patient.

Ruth 3:16-18

When Ruth came to her mother-in-law, Naomi asked, "How did it go, my daughter?" Then she told her everything Boaz had done for her [17]and added, "He gave me these six measures of barley, saying, 'Don't go back to your mother-in-law empty-handed.'" [18]Then Naomi said, "Wait, my daughter, until you find out what happens. For the man will not rest until the matter is settled today."

Boaz recognized the importance of showing family loyalty; he was committed to protecting Ruth. He did this appropriately by checking with the relative who was closest to her. He was secure enough to marry a foreigner. This security may have been due to the fact that his mother was also a foreigner, Rahab (Matt. 1:5).

Ruth 3:10-13

"The Lord bless you, my daughter," he replied. "This kindness is greater than that which you showed earlier: You have not run after the younger men, whether rich or poor. [11]And now, my daughter, don't be afraid. I will do for you all you ask. All my fellow townsmen know that you are a woman of noble character. [12]Although it is true that I am near of kin, there is a kinsman-redeemer nearer than I. [13]Stay here for the night, and in the morning if he wants to redeem, good; let him redeem. But if he is not willing, as surely as the Lord lives I will do it. Lie here until morning."

Ruth 4:1-13

Meanwhile Boaz went up to the town gate and sat there. When the kinsman–redeemer he had mentioned came along, Boaz said, "Come over here, my friend, and sit down." So he went over and sat down. [2]Boaz took ten of the elders of the town and said, "Sit here," and they did so. [3]Then he said to the kinsman-redeemer, "Naomi, who has come back from Moab, is selling the piece of land that belonged to our brother Elimelech. [4]I thought I should bring the matter to your attention and suggest that you buy it in the presence of these seated here and in the presence of the elders of my people. If you will redeem it, do so. But if you will not, tell me, so I will know. For no one has the right to do it except you, and I am next in line." "I will redeem it," he said. [5]Then Boaz said, "On the day you buy the land from Naomi and from Ruth the Moabitess, you acquire the dead man's widow, in order to maintain the name of the dead with his property."

[6]At this, the kinsman-redeemer said, "Then I cannot redeem it because I might endanger my own estate. You redeem it yourself. I cannot do it." [7](Now in earlier times in Israel, for the redemption and transfer of property to become final, one party took off his sandal and gave it to the other. This was the method of legalizing transactions in Israel.) [8]So the kinsman-redeemer said to Boaz, "Buy it yourself." And he removed his sandal. [9]Then Boaz announced to the elders and all the people, "Today you are witnesses that I have bought from Naomi all the property of Elimelech, Kilion and Mahlon. [10] I have also acquired Ruth the Moabitess, Mahlon's widow, as my wife, in order to maintain the name of the dead with his property, so that his name will not disappear from among his family or from the town records. Today you are witnesses!" [11]Then the elders and all those at the gate said, "We are witnesses. May the Lord make the woman who is coming into your home like Rachel and Leah, who together built up the house of Israel. May you have standing in Ephrathah and be famous in Bethlehem. [12] Through the offspring the Lord gives you by this young woman, may your family be

Ruth was more than a daughter-in-law to Naomi, and Naomi's child was more than a grandson, he was like a son to Ruth. The relationship as an adoptive parent includes the adoptee's spouse and children. Ruth was listed in the genealogy of Christ, though Naomi was not. This is an illustration of generational blessing.

like that of Perez, whom Tamar bore to Judah." [13]So Boaz took Ruth and she became his wife. Then he went to her, and the Lord enabled her to conceive, and she gave birth to a son.

Ruth 4:13-17

So Boaz took Ruth and she became his wife. Then he went to her, and the Lord enabled her to conceive, and she gave birth to a son. [14]The women said to Naomi: "Praise be to the Lord, who this day has not left you without a kinsman-redeemer. May he become famous throughout Israel! [15]He will renew your life and sustain you in your old age. For your daughter-in-law, who loves you and who is better to you than seven sons, has given him birth." [16]Then Naomi took the child, laid him in her lap and cared for him. [17]The women living there said, "Naomi has a son." And they named him Obed. He was the father of Jesse, the father of David.

Matthew 1:5

Salmon the father of Boaz, whose mother was Rahab, Boaz the father of Obed, whose mother was Ruth, Obed the father of Jesse,

Re-parenting can bring about the ability to dwell in faith, being sure and certain of what is unseen.

> Hebrews 11:1
> Now faith is being sure of what we hope for and certain of what we do not see.

Faith can only mature in the context of a spiritual relationship with our heavenly Father. Faith outside of relational context is only an informational concept which would not have the power to transform the individual and produce the fruit of the Spirit.

> Galatians 5:22-23
> But the fruit of the Spirit is love, joy, peace, patience, kindness, goodness, faithfulness, [23]gentleness and self-control. Against such things there is no law.

The physical and emotional needs of an individual, contingent on the age when those needs are met, facilitate and intensify the secure base attachment. Developmental processes in the first twelve months of life are essential to the development of a secure base attachment and directly correlate to spiritual development. Experiencing the security of being held as an infant will enable the secure base attached person to enjoy being in God's presence.

> Psalm 16:11
> You have made known to me the path of life; you will fill me with joy in your presence, with eternal pleasures at your right hand.

> Psalm 21:6
> Surely you have granted him eternal blessings and made him glad with the joy of your presence.

Ministering to a child's needs physically and emotionally during a time of distress induces calmness and assurance. As a child of God, a secure base attached person can take his feelings of fear and go to God for comfort knowing that He is always available.

> Psalm 18:16
> He reached down from on high and took hold of me; he drew me out of deep waters.

> Psalm 73:23
> Yet I am always with you; you hold me by my right hand.

> Isaiah 41:13
> For I am the Lord, your God, who takes hold of your right hand and says to you, Do not fear; I will help you.

Infants are able to express their needs by body language, crying, vocalizations, and words, and in so doing expect those needs to be met, this is the basis for secure base attached adults to develop an interactive prayer life. They expect God to hear them and meet their needs.

> Psalm 4:3
> Know that the Lord has set apart the godly for himself; the Lord will hear when I call to him

> Psalm 5:3
> In the morning, O Lord, you hear my voice; in the morning I lay my requests before you and wait in expectation.

> Psalm 38:15
> I wait for you, O Lord; you will answer, O Lord my God.

Psalm 55:2

Hear me and answer me. My thoughts trouble me and I am distraught

Psalm 66:19

but God has surely listened and heard my voice in prayer.

Psalm 116:1

I love the Lord, for he heard my voice; he heard my cry for mercy.

Infants as young as two days old show preference for their mother's voice.[68] By five months infants can recognize their name in the midst of background noise.[69] As an adoptive parent, pray that your child begins to recognize your voice. Recognizing the voice of one who meets needs as an infant provides a basis for recognizing God's voice as He meets needs thus providing a secure relationship with God.

John 10:16

I have other sheep that are not of this sheep pen. I must bring them also. They too will listen to my voice, and there shall be one flock and one shepherd.

John 10:4

When he has brought out all his own, he goes on ahead of them, and his sheep follow him because they know his voice.

---

68 C. Moon and W. P. Fifer. "Syllables as signals for 2-day-old-infants." *Infant Behavior and Development*,13 (July-September 1990): 352-362.

69 R. S. Newman. "The Cocktail Party Effect in Infants Revisited: Listening to One's Name in Noise." *Developmental Psychology*, 41 (March 2005): 352-362.

Infants are able to experience and express enjoyment. Spontaneous smiling occurs in infants during sleep twenty-four hours after birth.[70] As adults they learn the importance of praise and that the joy of the Lord is their strength.

I Chronicles 29:22

They ate and drank with great joy in the presence of the Lord that day. Then they acknowledged Solomon son of David as king a second time, anointing him before the Lord to be ruler and Zadok to be priest.

Nehemiah 8:10

Nehemiah said, "Go and enjoy choice food and sweet drinks, and send some to those who have nothing prepared. This day is sacred to our Lord. Do not grieve, for the joy of the Lord is your strength."

Psalm 28:7

The Lord is my strength and my shield; my heart trusts in him, and I am helped. My heart leaps for joy and I will give thanks to him in song.

Infants respond to emotions of others, enabling them as secure base attached adults to develop empathy and to understand that God has empathy for their emotions.

Hebrews 13:3

Remember those in prison as if you were their fellow prisoners, and those who are mistreated as if you yourselves were suffering.

---

70 K. Kawakami, K. Takai-Kawakami, M. Tomonaga, J. Suzuki, T. Tomiyo, and T. Okai. "Origins of smile and laughter: A preliminary study." *Early Human Development*, 82 (2006): 61-66.

Romans 12:15

Rejoice with those who rejoice; mourn with those who mourn.

Parenting takes time, it is not always convenient. Teaching moments cannot always be scheduled in advance, so the parent must be alert for opportunities to communicate, and the more time families spend together, the more opportunities they will find. Model the gospel, become a living testimony.

1 Thessalonians 1:5-7

because our gospel came to you not simply with words, but also with power, with the Holy Spirit and with deep conviction. You know how we lived among you for your sake. ⁶You became imitators of us and of the Lord; in spite of severe suffering, you welcomed the message with the joy given by the Holy Spirit. ⁷And so you became a model to all the believers in Macedonia and Achaia.

1 Peter 5:3

not lording it over those entrusted to you, but being examples to the flock.

The daily tasks of living are as much a ministry to the Lord as a public ministry. It is important to take care of both the physical and spiritual needs of the child. Believers should not compartmentalize their lives. Children dictate some needs, but parents dictate how those needs are met. When hungry, the child cries and the parent feeds him; fatigue indicates the need for rest. However, the child is only aware of the discomfort, he does not always understand what he needs, nor does he know how to meet his own needs. Adoptive parents need to be aware that the child may not always be able to articulate his needs stemming from a break in bonding. Intercessory prayer is necessary to receive discernment for revelation in order to address that need.

Children are born with certain temperaments and personality characteristics that need to be molded. Parents need to work within the framework of the child's needs and God-given attributes.

Proverbs 20:27 (AMP)

The spirit of man [that factor in human personality which proceeds immediately from God] is the lamp of the Lord, searching all his innermost parts.

Ephesians 3:16 (AMP)

May He grant you out of the rich treasury of His glory to be strengthened and reinforced with mighty power in the inner man by the [Holy] Spirit [Himself indwelling your innermost being and personality].

Colossians 1:4 (AMP)

For we have heard of your faith in Christ Jesus [the leaning of your entire human personality on Him in absolute trust and confidence in His power, wisdom, and goodness] and of the love which you [have and show] for all the saints (God's consecrated ones),

Personality traits and gifts all have positive and negative aspects. Being laidback may be perceived as having difficulty with self-motivation. Leadership qualities may, until maturation, appear as bossiness. Discernment may appear as judgmental. Compassion may lead to fear of confrontation. Each child comes with a different response to their break in attachment as well as their ability to reform a new attachment. As a parent it is imperative to be consistent in meeting the child's physical and emotional needs.

Chapter 14

Steps Of Spiritual Re-parenting

The ultimate objective of spiritual re-parenting is to help the adopted child feel more comfortable in situations with emotional (horizontal relationship) and spiritual (vertical relationship) interaction. The goal is to help this child develop a close, nurturing relationship with friends and family, and the ability to ask for what he needs and refuse what he does not want, without acute feelings of shame and guilt.

Make a list of challenging behaviors that impact the horizontal relationship and describe how they are a hindrance to spiritual growth. Spend time fasting and praying about the issues on the list to discern the roots of such difficulties. Upon receiving insight to the list of problems, compare this to what you know about your child, seeking confirmation and affirmation. Utilize the worksheet below.

Problem Behaviors

1)_____

2)_____

3)_____

Impact on Relationships

1)_____

2)_____

3)_____

Impact on Spiritual Maturity

1)_____

2)_____

3)_____

Develop a clear strategy for psychospiritual intervention. The spiritual parent provides guidance in this effort and must maintain positive prayer support at all times.

> **2 Timothy 1:3**
> I thank God, whom I serve, as my forefathers did, with a clear conscience, as night and day I constantly remember you in my prayers.

During this task, the child may feel extremely threatened, vulnerable, and subjected to "spiritual oppression." Therefore, the parent must provide spiritual covering to prevent the child from entering into acute clinical depression due to the prolonged experience of "spiritual oppression" and/or psychological distress. The overt manifestation of "spiritual oppression" is essentially similar to clinical depression. The main technical difference is the etiology or cause. From a psychological standpoint, distress tends to occur due to acute awareness of what was lacking in one's life due to the inappropriate parenting the individual received. This would tend to evoke regret, anger, hurt, or projection of blame onto the biological parent. From the standpoint of spirituality, the enemy would be motivated in preventing believers from developing a mature faith-relationship with the heavenly Father.

Ephesians 6:12

For our struggle is not against flesh and blood, but against the rulers, against the authorities, against the powers of this dark world and against the spiritual forces of evil in the heavenly realms.

The following outline offers general concepts for psychospiritual re-parenting.

1) Decide the primary objective of the intervention:

- What problematical thing [behavior] is the child doing?

- What is the frequency of this problem?

- How does this hinder intervention and deliverance?

- When does this problem typically show itself?

2) Develop a psychospiritual support system for yourself and your child. Scriptures mandate to not forsake fellowship.

Hebrews 10:25

Let us not give up meeting together, as some are in the habit of doing, but let us encourage one another—and all the more as you see the Day approaching.

Through the fellowship both child and the adopted parent will receive encouragement to continue their respective journey into spiritual maturity, in spite of trials and tribulations encountered throughout this journey.

Matthew 18:16

But if he will not listen, take one or two others along, so that 'every matter may be established by the testimony of two or three witnesses.'

Matthew 18:19-20

"Again, I tell you that if two of you on earth agree about anything you ask for, it will be done for you by my Father in heaven. [20]For where two or three come together in my name, there am I with them."

Titus 2:4-5

Then they can train the younger women to love their husbands and children, [5]to be self-controlled and pure, to be busy at home, to be kind, and to be subject to their husbands, so that no one will malign the word of God.

- Gather information from the people who support you regarding factors that appear to be affecting the child's behavior without disclosing any confidential information.

- Talk with the child about his emotional state and frame of mind before, during, and after behavioral incidents.

3) Learn to give effective feedback.

- As you give feedback to your child, be specific, simple, and timely.

- Pray for God's favorable timing as to when you should give feedback.

Matthew 10:19

But when they arrest you, do not worry about what to say or how to say it. At that time you will be given what to say,

Matthew 24:45

"Who then is the faithful and wise servant, whom the master has put in charge of the servants in his household to give them their food at the proper time?

Luke 12:12

for the Holy Spirit will teach you at that time what you should say."

Romans 5:6

You see, at just the right time, when we were still powerless, Christ died for the ungodly.

Proverbs 25:11

A word aptly spoken is like apples of gold in settings of silver.

- Provide concrete examples of your observations.

- Tailor your words to the child's personality and communication style.

- Be aware of your demeanor; do not act angry, disappointed, or judgmental.

Matthew 7:1-2

"Do not judge, or you too will be judged. ²For in the same way you judge others, you will be judged, and with the measure you use, it will be measured to you.

Romans 14:4

Who are you to judge someone else's servant? To his own master he stands or falls. And he will stand, for the Lord is able to make him stand.

Romans 14:10

You, then, why do you judge your brother? Or why do you look down on your brother? For we will all stand before God's judgment seat.

Colossians 2:16

Therefore do not let anyone judge you by what you eat or drink, or with regard to a religious festival, a New Moon celebration or a Sabbath day.

I Corinthians 4:14

I am not writing this to shame you, but to warn you, as my dear children.

Colossians 3:12

Therefore, as God's chosen people, holy and dearly loved, clothe yourselves with compassion, kindness, humility, gentleness and patience.

- Be supportive, compassionate, and understanding.

- Request age appropriate feedback from the child during the discussion. Use this opportunity to learn from each other. You can learn how to be a better parent and how to better minister to your child's needs.

- Be a source of consistent, positive psychospiritual support.

4) Be a source of encouragement.

I Thessalonians 5:11

Therefore encourage one another and build each other up, just as in fact you are doing.

I Thessalonians 5:14

And we urge you, brothers, warn those who are idle, encourage the timid, help the weak, be patient with everyone.

2 Timothy 4:2

Preach the Word; be prepared in season and out of season; correct, rebuke and encourage—with great patience and careful instruction.

Titus 2:15

These, then, are the things you should teach. Encourage and rebuke with all authority. Do not let anyone despise you.

Hebrews 3:13

But encourage one another daily, as long as it is called Today, so that none of you may be hardened by sin's deceitfulness.

- Be emotionally and spiritually aware of your reaction to your child's behavior. You will not be effective if your reaction pushes the child away.

- Be available to listen. When the child wants to talk, be emotionally ready and available. Do not miss an opportunity for the child to experience "catharsis" by letting go and opening up.

- Help the child see how the situation effects him and his life. Typically, people with insecure attachment have difficulty acquiring insight into their predicaments.

- Be a constant, dependable source of emotional and spiritual nurturing. Without being judgmental, allow the child to express dread, fear, and anxiety. Do not be intimidated or feel guilty if the problem is beyond your ability to process.

This is a relationship process, and not informational impartation to make the individual cognitively aware of causes of their problems, typical of counseling intervention. In the process of re-parenting the individual experiences being fed both emotionally and spiritually, thereby developing the capacity to feel secure.

Chapter 15

Why Adults Need Spiritual Parents

In the church, attachment disorders in ministers can affect an entire congregation. Scores of books written by people in the New Apostolic Movement encourage ministers to build effective alliances within the fivefold gifts of ministry. Listed in Ephesians 4:11, these gifts include apostles, prophets, evangelists, pastors, and teachers. All of these gifts are needed within a congregation. To develop alliances with people who have different ministry gifts requires the ability to have "object relationship" capacity. Object relationship is the ability to form reciprocal (give and take) relationships. If pastors or ministers suffer from some form of attachment dysfunction due to being inadequately parented, they will have profound difficulty when it comes to recruiting "ministry partners."

Except for the gift of evangelism, all ministerial gifts within the context of a fivefold ministry depend on close interaction with others. Ministers who suffer from attachment dysfunction find it difficult to accept authority, because they fear being abandoned or taken advantage of. This makes it difficult for them to establish a trusting relationship with God, and with other ministers and helpers. Due to this fear, such ministers find it difficult to make a long-term commitment to their communities.

Attachment dysfunction also poses problems for converts to the church who need mentoring and for members who have been believers for some time. During the mentoring process, the minister or other church members teach belief systems, behavior, and other aspects of spiritual life. Mentoring becomes a challenge when the convert or longtime member has experienced attachment dysfunction due to a negative parent-child relationship or traumatic events.

An Example of Secure Base Attachment

Tom came to his calling in his late thirties after a successful career in sales and marketing. He graduated from college with a degree in Business Administration. His employer recognized his worth and Tom received several well deserved promotions. When he became a licensed minister, he was assigned to a church of twenty members; this was a congregation that was dying a slow death. The denominational superintendent gave this novice minister three to four years to bring life back otherwise, the church would be closed and its membership would merge with another church in a different town. In fact, Tom had to work part-time in a regular job to support his family, since the church did not have enough members to pay him an adequate salary.

Being trained in sales and marketing as well as in organizational dynamics, Tom immediately recognized the sense of helplessness his congregation exhibited. He spent many hours truly getting to know the psychospiritual needs of his people. He learned that most of his members did not know who they were in Christ, or more importantly what their divine purpose and calling was in God's Kingdom in their community. For the next two years, Tom fostered a covenant relationship with his congregation on a daily basis instead of the typical Wednesday and Sunday interactions. As the relationships grew between this minister and his congregation, the love matured and gave birth to vibrant, active church members. He scheduled regular times not only to pray and nurture their spiritual needs, but also to sponsor fun activities between his family and every family unit in his congregation. During this process, he bonded with each family. He handled problems in a consistent manner and always expressed appreciation (both publicly and in private) toward his congregation. He did not hesitate to admit his own shortcomings and would ask for help in overcoming certain problems. He was willing to be vulnerable. This minister shepherded his congregational flock back to life by spiritually re-parenting them, one family unit at the time. As the congregational family unit became psychospiritually mature, they were able to reach out to other families in the community and replicate the nurturing interaction they learned from their pastor.

When believers are able to fully appreciate their identity in Christ, their psychospiritual capacity to form ministerial relationships is enhanced. As vertical relationships with God and horizontal relationships with re-parenting by spiritual adopted parents matures, fivefold ministerial gifting is enhanced. People who have reached this point in their spiritual lives become conduits of God's blessings for the entire congregation. The role models they provide for vertical and horizontal relationships will help create a healthy church.

Anxious Ambivalent Attachment

Individuals with anxious ambivalent attachment who graduate from Bible school and are assigned to minister to a church will invest most of their efforts in teaching and preaching. Personal relationships stay in the background. During times of congregational needs, these ministers are typically not emotionally available and tend to wait in the wings until the crisis subsides. They might provide prayer and cite appropriate Scriptures, but mercy, compassion, and empathy will be lacking. Any criticism they receive will be personalized, and blame will be projected elsewhere. When the elder board begins to expect ministerial program development, the level of performance anxiety intensifies. Conflicts develop between the pastor and anyone who places expectations upon him. Vertical relationships are an issue, because the pastor's parenting was inconsistent and intermittently unresponsive. He cannot truly accept the fact that God the Father is a loving, kind, merciful, and an eternally loving God who will never abandon him. Living on faith to have their needs be met by God is so anxiety provoking it creates anguish. The mandate of "Be anxious for nothing" (Phil. 4:6) is a foreign emotional experience. For these ministers, childhood experience with caregivers was so unreliable that as adults they still hold an emotional fear of being abandoned.

An Example of Anxious Ambivalent Attachment

Being retained by a district superintendent to assess an unusual pattern of membership attrition at a particular church, interviews were conducted with all the elected board members, the senior pastor, the associate pastor, and the salaried support staff. In addition, a questionnaire was sent out to the volunteer staff: Sunday school teachers, members of the worship team, and cell group leaders. The results indicated the senior pastor had a leadership style of "micro-managing" all aspects of the church ministry program. Both salaried and volunteer staff members expressed a profound level of frustration. If a ministry program was not successful, the staff assigned to that program felt blamed and criticized by the senior pastor. On the other hand, if the program was successful, the senior pastor would replace the person in charge and take over the program himself. The program would then deteriorate within six months. Within three years of this pastor's arrival at this church, membership dropped by 52 percent.

Since all Sunday morning sermons are audio taped, it was requested that copies of sermons for the past eighteen months be made available for review. Content-based analysis reflected the senior pastor's progressive level of insecurity, inadequacy, and frustration. Conflict between the elected board members and the senior pastor intensified. The senior pastor attempted to remedy the problem by doing a series of Sunday morning sermons on "Authority and Submission." His micro-management style grew in intensity to the point of critiquing a prayer given during a Sunday morning service. During the Wednesday night Bible study or in his adult Sunday school, if any participant commented on anything, the senior pastor would have the last authoritative statement. The senior pastor recruited and surrounded himself with "young Christians and passive adults" who did not question his authority and would implement his mandates. The senior pastor was asked if he would be willing to participate in a "clinical interview" in contrast to an organizational assessment in which the assessment findings were shared and concerns about his management style explained.

This pastor's oldest brother was senior pastor of a large church in the Midwest with a membership of approximately a thousand people. The second oldest brother was a missionary who planted at least five churches. Being the youngest of three children, this man originally pursued a career in the secular world until his late twenties. He described his relationship with his father during his developmental and formative years as strained, due to his father's lack of physical and emotional availability. The father was a typical minister who gave his "all" to the congregation. The two older brothers expressed the desire to be in the ministry early on in their adolescent years, and therefore they received more attention from their father. The father would take the two oldest sons on short mission trips and let them help with his evangelistic outreach ministry; therefore, the relationship between the older sons and father grew closer. The youngest son became more distant from the father. The mother was physically and emotionally available, but her determination to have the youngest son pursue a ministerial career hindered their relationship. The pastor grew up thinking parental love was conditional, though he did not rebel during his adolescent years.

At the end of the clinical interview, feedback was given to the pastor and his attachment style "anxious ambivalent" was addressed. Being bright and psychologically minded, he agreed to psychospiritual counseling. Within three months of the counseling effort, he openly apologized to the congregation. He telephoned each member who had left the church and explained that his lack of awareness was the reason they left. The pastor requested an opportunity to participate in conflict resolution with those members who left the church and to establish a covenant relationship with them, regardless of whether or not they chose to come back.

An Example of Avoidant Attachment

In twenty years of ministerial consultation there has been only one ordained minister who fell into the category of avoidant attachment. He lasted less than two years in each of the several churches where he served as a senior pastor. During his tenure, the churches experienced mass exodus of membership. The congregations' primary complaints about their pastor centered on his lack of warmth, his social evasiveness, and his abrasive, angry response to church members' personal problems. Like this unfortunate minister, people with avoidant attachment style react with intense fear when faced with demands for emotional closeness; they doubt their ability to provide emotional sustenance. The congregation perceives this behavior as indifference to their need for pastoral care. More importantly, this type of pastor may commit spiritual abuse as a result of their egocentricity and narcissistic tendencies. Spiritual abuse may be an actively overt or passively subtle act of influencing individuals that their disobedience or contrary life style to the teaching being provided is at unacceptable levels; therefore, will be punished by God and preclude entrance to heaven.[71]

An Example of Disorganized Attachment

If by remote chance people with disorganized attachment become involved in the ministry, the risk to the congregation is enormous. These individuals tend to be sociopathic and will probably use the church for personal gain. Having evaluated ministers referred by their district superintendent or district supervisor due to "moral failure" one is able to see the effects of disorganized attachment disorder on personality development. One case involved embezzlement of church funds. Every time the pastor was unable to meet his financial obligation to creditors, he would take whatever amount he needed to pay to his bills. The rationale given was, "I'm making the sacrifice to be their pastor

---

71 B. C. Purcell. "Spiritual abuse." *American Journal of Hospice and Palliative Medicine*, 15 (1998): 227-31.

and they are not paying me enough. Besides, I'm protecting them by not embarrassing them. Who would want to come to this church if the public found out their pastor couldn't pay his bills because they are not paying him an adequate salary?" This type of individual's super-ego (conscience) is so underdeveloped that they tend to not experience any sense of guilt for their wrongdoing.

Individuals with disorganized attachment are not very common within the ministry. Even though the majority are bright and are able to meet the academic demands of Bible school, the ministerial practicum and close supervision tends to discourage this type of individual from pursuing ministry as a profession. The concept of providing endless compassion, self-sacrificial attitude to the congregants, and minimal financial compensation would aggravate the sense of traumatic victimization. This would compel them to seek out a different vocational endeavor that would enhance their sense of entitlement and reinforce the need to be in control to minimize any victimization or perceived victimization. The perception or any experience of being marginalized would magnify previous experiences of traumatic abandonment. Ministers are often unappreciated by their congregation in spite of working an average of fifty to sixty hours a week. This would evoke anger due to the perception and interpretation of being taken advantage of. This anger would in turn lead to inappropriate behavior such as financial mismanagement of church funds, sexual boundary intrusion, or under productivity.

Spiritual Parents

Having church members who are willing to become adopted spiritual parents is the most effective way to develop an emotionally healthy church. To develop trust, the spiritual parent needs to meet the adult spiritual child's basic physical and emotional needs; helping with basic life skills, e.g., paying bills, hygiene, parenting of their own children, preparing meals, cleaning, cooking, social skills, job skills, etc. Re-parenting must not be done at the expense of one's own immediate family. God has given parents the primary responsibility of raising their children. Do not place them at risk.

For best results, spiritual adoptive adult children should be at a different stage of life than one's own children, so no one feels competition for love. Not all spiritual mentoring relationships need be parent/child. Family relationships are multilevel and are important on all levels. For someone who is the same age as your children, you might form an aunt or uncle type of relationship without the risk of fostering unhealthy competition within your family unit. In addition, when becoming a spiritual parent, the family of the spiritually adopted adult child should not be overlooked. Paul had a relationship with Timothy's mother and grandmother.

Just as in parenting, spiritual re-parenting brings little glamour or recognition. The investment of parenting is not seen as vital by many individuals; therefore, the investment in spiritually adopted adult children is often seen as over involvement. More often than not Christians tend to opine that cell group, Bible study, spiritual retreats, or short-term mission trips are enough to bring individuals to spiritual maturity. This is a long-term process. The primary focus of psychospiritual re-parenting is to transform dysfunctional behavior into normal behavior and enhance spiritual awareness so the adopted adult child can enjoy a full, loving relationship with God.

Who to Re-Parent

One must be very selective in whom to re-parent. Old Testament examples include Moses and Joshua, Elijah and Elisha. New Testament examples include Paul and Timothy, Paul and Titus, Barnabas and Paul. Note that those chosen to be re-parented had a lot of potential. Moses and Elijah each had only one person they were re-parenting and they, Joshua and Elisha, already had a commitment to God. Timothy was committed to God as well, and even though he had a believing mother and grandmother, because he had a Greek father (unbelieving father) he still needed a spiritual father in his life. Titus also had a commitment to God.

2 Timothy 1:5

I have been reminded of your sincere faith, which first lived in your grandmother Lois and in your mother Eunice and, I am persuaded, now lives in you also.

Acts 16:1

He came to Derbe and then to Lystra, where a disciple named Timothy lived, whose mother was a Jewess and a believer, but whose father was a Greek.

Titus 1:4

To Titus, my true son in our common faith: Grace and peace from God the Father and Christ Jesus our Savior.

If, as seems common, people choose to re-parent those most in need there is a high rate of burnout. If the person is not willing to change then re-parenting is useless. Paul did not choose to re-parent Hymenaeus and Alexander. Because of their unwillingness to repent they were expelled from the church in order to bring them to repentance.

1 Timothy 1:20

Among them are Hymenaeus and Alexander, whom I have handed over to Satan to be taught not to blaspheme.

Jesus chose the original twelve from people who were hard working. The disciples were teachable.

Matthew 4:18-19

As Jesus was walking beside the Sea of Galilee, he saw two brothers, Simon called Peter and his brother Andrew. They were casting a net into the lake, for they were fishermen. [19]"Come, follow me," Jesus said, "and I will make you fishers of men."

Matthew 10:2-4

These are the names of the twelve apostles: first, Simon (who is called Peter) and his brother Andrew; James son of Zebedee, and his brother John; ³Philip and Bartholomew; Thomas and Matthew the tax collector; James son of Alphaeus, and Thaddaeus; ⁴Simon the Zealot and Judas Iscariot, who betrayed him.

Colossians 4:14

Our dear friend Luke, the doctor, and Demas send greetings.

Matthew 11:1

After Jesus had finished instructing his twelve disciples, he went on from there to teach and preach in the towns of Galilee.

Matthew 13:10-11

The disciples came to him and asked, "Why do you speak to the people in parables?" ¹¹He replied, "The knowledge of the secrets of the kingdom of heaven has been given to you, but not to them.

Matthew 13:16

But blessed are your eyes because they see, and your ears because they hear.

The spiritual adult child has a responsibility to be accountable to the spiritual parent. If they choose not to be accountable, the spiritual parent must be willing to perform intercessory prayer for them. Be aware of your limits in agreeing to re-parent.

People, like King Saul, who have an unrepentant attitude toward God will have greater difficulty developing a mature spiritual life. Furthermore, unrepentance for "generational sins" also is a significant barrier to one's spiritual growth and maturity. The spiritual parent must be aware of their own agenda. They must be willing to invest time in intercessory prayer in order to discover God's ultimate objective in that person's life rather than making assumptions based on superficial "discernment" of that person's needs.

The following is an illustration of this concept. An extremely needy woman in her twenties was being spiritually mothered by an older woman. This young woman lived in filth and clutter. Due to carelessness she had a fire in her apartment. Her spiritual mother told her that many of her things had smoke damage, when they did not, just so she could get her to throw the items away. In so doing the young woman threw out many books and dishes which did not belong to her. Temporarily her apartment was less cluttered but this did nothing to solve the underlying problem. In fact, it compounded it as she discovered the deception of her spiritual mother; thus, further exacerbating her trust issues. There are several basic underlying principles to be aware of. First, this young woman's issues were beyond the spiritual mother's ability, second, the spiritual mother was only dealing with surface issues as opposed to root causes, and third, in her haste to solve surface issues the spiritual mother became just one more relationship which victimized the young woman. Only intercessory prayer for the spiritually adopted child and asking for divine guidance for them will enable God's agenda to be accomplished.

If the spiritually adopted adult child needs to develop in the area of forgiveness, teach him to identify the problem and the process of forgiveness. Provide practical guidelines on what to do and how to respond. Knowing the Word is not enough; he must learn to apply the Word. However, as with the hungry child dictating the need for food, the parent dictates the type of food. With the spiritual adult child limits and boundaries must be set by the spiritual parent until they are ready to set their own.

A child's growth and maturation depend upon internal and external influences, and so it is with the spiritual adult child. No set pattern or formula will work for every person. Learning to walk requires at least half a dozen underlying steps: head control, the ability to balance, sit, stand, and finally take that first step. Parents are not concerned when the child first begins to stand and then promptly falls when he realizes he is standing. Nor do they concern themselves each time the child falls as he learns to walk. Instead, they provide a safe place for him to practice, and they focus on his successes.

Re-parenting also requires many underlying steps. First and foremost is falling in love with the spiritual adult child, creating a firm foundation of commitment. Intercede for him and learn his background. Meet his basic needs in order to develop trust. Be committed to intercession, even if he leaves the relationship. Re-parenting means never giving up. It is a lifetime commitment. However, the relationship should change over time, from a parent/child relationship into a covenant relationship. At first the relationship will be intense and time consuming. A newborn has constant needs, as he matures, it will become less time intense and gradually evolve into a relationship based on respect, and lastly to an empty nest. The spiritual parent should be ready and willing to let go when the time comes.

Parenting will bring criticism from other churchgoers who do not understand the adopted spiritual adult child, often the "child" is criticized instead of the parent. Those who are mature do not usually fit in well. They are shunned because others do not want to confront their own psychological shortcomings. Paul gave specific instructions to Timothy concerning what to teach; however, Timothy's authority was questioned because of his youth. Paul told him to not let others despise him because of his youth.

I Timothy 1:3-4

As I urged you when I went into Macedonia, stay there in Ephesus so that you may command certain men not to teach false doctrines any longer 4nor to devote themselves to myths and endless genealogies. These promote controversies rather than God's work—which is by faith.

I Timothy 3:14-15

Although I hope to come to you soon, I am writing you these instructions so that, ¹⁵ if I am delayed, you will know how people ought to conduct themselves in God's household, which is the church of the living God, the pillar and foundation of the truth.

I Timothy 4:6

If you point these things out to the brothers, you will be a good minister of Christ Jesus, brought up in the truths of the faith and of the good teaching that you have followed.

I Timothy 4:11-13

Command and teach these things. ¹²Don't let anyone look down on you because you are young, but set an example for the believers in speech, in life, in love, in faith and in purity. ¹³Until I come, devote yourself to the public reading of Scripture, to preaching and to teaching.

It is essential for the spiritual adoptive parent to not only understand their responsibilities; they must have some practical knowledge as how to facilitate spiritual re-parenting.

Spiritual Parenting of an Adult

This relationship goes beyond acquaintance, it develops into a true familial relationship with devotion and loyalty to one another.	Romans 12:10 Be devoted to one another in brotherly love. Honor one another above yourselves. Romans 12:4-5 Just as each of us has one body with many members, and these members do not all have the

	same function, [5]so in Christ we who are many form one body, and each member belongs to all the others. 1 Corinthians 10:16-17 Is not the cup of thanksgiving for which we give thanks a participation in the blood of Christ? And is not the bread that we break a participation in the body of Christ? [17]Because there is one loaf, we, who are many, are one body, for we all partake of the one loaf.
Re-parenting involves financial commitment, a sharing of resources.	1 John 3:16-18 This is how we know what love is: Jesus Christ laid down his life for us. And we ought to lay down our lives for our brothers. [17]If anyone has material possessions and sees his brother in need but has no pity on him, how can the love of God be in him? [18]Dear children, let us not love with words or tongue but with actions and in truth. Acts 2:44-45 All the believers were together and had everything in common. [45]Selling their possessions and goods, they gave to anyone as he had need.

Steps of Spiritual Re-parenting

Developing a clear strategy for psychospiritual intervention is the mutual responsibility of both the spiritual adoptee and the spiritually adopted parent. The spiritual parent provides guidance in this effort and must maintain positive prayer support at all times. The support people should be the same gender as the adoptee, to prevent the wrong type of emotional attachment. This is not the time for romantic involvement.

Paul was a spiritual parent to Timothy and Titus.

> I Corinthians 4:14-15
>
> I am not writing this to shame you, but to warn you, as my dear children. [15]Even though you have ten thousand guardians in Christ, you do not have many fathers, for in Christ Jesus I became your father through the gospel

There are several things to consider when choosing an adoptive parent. Has the adopted parent successfully raised his or her biological children? Having troubled children should not automatically disqualify a parent, but the adoptee should pray for knowledge and discernment, asking if the parent has matured both emotionally and spiritually in the Lord. Again, Eli is an example of a spiritual parent who was not successful in parenting his own children.

The following variables are factors that should be discussed in formalizing the re-parenting relationship. The items delineated below are reciprocal responsibilities that need to be processed to be successful in re-parenting so that both adoptee and adopted parent are fully aware of the expectation from each other. The key concept is in "FORMALIZING" re-parenting due process relationship thereby eradicating the negative consequences of inappropriate parenting. In an informal re-parenting relationship, the expectation would be haphazard, and in most cases if there is any expectation imposed by the adopted parent on the adult adoptee, typically there would be resistance which would strain the relationship. A good illustration is the movie *Karate Kid*, whereby Mr. Miyagi agreed to teach the young student without discussing the due process. The student became angry after several days of doing "chores" since he was not made aware of the due process of learning martial arts. This list should be processed prior to implementation of a formal re-parenting effort.

a) **Negotiation phase:** (expectation) If rules/expectations are not put into place formally, they will form over time. Rules form from tradition, formal organization, and by lack of enforcing any type of rule.

b) **Duration:** Parenting responsibilities are a lifetime obligation, but they should diminish as the adult adoptee matures, lest co-dependency develop. Developmental autonomy and spiritual maturity should determine the intensity of parenting.

c) **Activities:** This should include both formal activities, such as Bible study, praying together, or financial planning, and informal activities, such as shopping, meals, and movies. Many adults have difficulty with daily living skills, including meal planning, holding a job, and budgeting. The activities should range from concrete weekly meetings and assignments to less formal family interaction.

d) **Frequency:** Weekly meetings will progress to less frequent and less scheduled interaction as the adoptee matures.

e) **Accountability:** (reciprocal) Both parties must keep their commitments. The parent is accountable to the adult child to provide what was negotiated.

In recruiting an adopted spiritual parent, the individual should interview the potential adopted parent. Some questions are as follows:

1) How often do you pray for your children? Duration?

2) How do you pray for your children?

3) Do you practice fasting and praying for your children?

4) How do you resolve conflict with your children?

5) How do express love and affection for your children?

6) In hindsight, what are some of the hindrances you experienced in effectively parenting your children?

7) Do you provide intercessory prayer covering for your children daily? Weekly? Monthly?

8) Do you share your faults and shortcomings with your children?

9) Do you have formal training in spiritual warfare?

10) Do you covet compassion and mercy to be increased in your life daily?

11) Do you have a support system?

The primary emphasis is the spiritual maturity of the adopted parent. If the age difference is significant, at least twenty years, the gender issue becomes irrelevant. On the other hand, if the age difference is under ten years, ideally same sex is highly recommended. Personality compatibility is not is major factor provided that spiritual maturity is obviously present. Individuals who manifest spiritual maturity tend to walk under the prompting of the Holy Spirit and therefore are able to minimize the impact of their psychological shortcomings that could negatively influence their ministry responsibilities. Spiritual maturity tends to equate to psychological health.

A faith covenant is a tangible way to formalize the spiritual adoption process.

Faith Covenant

We, the undersigned pledge to provide each other with intercessory prayer covering that we may both receive revelation from our heavenly Father to facilitate accomplishing our respective responsibilities to each other. As an adult adoptee I will be receptive to the teaching and admonishment of my adopted parent. As an adoptive parent I will be cognizant of my responsibilities to raise my adopted adult child in the ways of righteousness.

_____

Adult Adoptee   Date

_____

Adoptive Parent   Date

Conclusion

Spiritual adoption is not a program, it is a human relationship based on religious principles and supported by God. Forming this relationship will enhance the spiritual maturation of both the adult child and the spiritually adopted parent. In the context of human relationship the impact on each other is reciprocal. The process of spiritual parenting compels the spiritually adopted parent to seek out the Holy Spirit for anointing and guidance in teaching and disciplining the spiritually adopted adult child in the path of righteousness. As the adult adoptee matures in the Lord, this overt behavior is witnessed by the spiritually adopted parent thereby becoming a blessing to the spiritually adopted parent, fully realizing that the time invested in prayer and parenting effort is a ministry in itself.

Proverbs 22:6

Train up a child in the way he should go: and when he is old, he will not depart from it.

There may be times of trial and tribulation in re-parenting the adult child, in the same manner that our Lord and Savior was subjected to the same challenge of disciplining the apostles early on.

Ephesians 3:14-21

For this reason I kneel before the Father, [15]from whom his whole family in heaven and on earth derives its name. [16]I pray that out of his glorious riches he may strengthen you with power through his Spirit in your inner being, [17]so that Christ may dwell in your hearts through faith. And I pray that you, being rooted and established in love, [18]may have power, together with all the saints, to grasp how wide and long and high and deep is the love of Christ, [19]and to know this love that surpasses knowledge—that you may be filled to the measure of all the fullness of God. [20]Now to him who is able to do immeasurably more than all we ask or imagine, according to his power that is at work within us, [21]to him be glory in the church and in Christ Jesus throughout all generations, for ever and ever! Amen.

**Intermedia
Publishing Group**

Publishing That Works For You

Do you need a speaker?

Do you want Rick and Sharon Ascano to speak to your group or event? Then contact Larry Davis at: (623) 337-8710 or email: ldavis@intermediapr.com or use the contact form at: www.intermediapr.com.

Whether you want to purchase bulk copies of *Spiritual Adoption* or buy another book for a friend, get it now at: www.imprbooks.com.